Who Were You Yesterday?

Breaunna H. Daniels

ISBN 978-1-64349-014-4 (paperback)
ISBN 978-1-64349-016-8 (hardcover)
ISBN 978-1-64349-015-1 (digital)

Christian Faith Publishing, Inc.
832 Park Avenue
Meadville, PA 16335
www.christianfaithpublishing.com

Photography by: Carissa Glanton (Diamond Eyez Photography)

Make up by: Diana Torres (Dilightfull Expressions)

Printed in the United States of America

Dedication

To my Heavenly Father, Jesus Christ!

From my beginning to my ending, God already knew how He was going to use me for His kingdom. This book will allow me to fulfill the purpose that God has for me. I am destined for greatness! All glory and honor goes to Him!

"No eye has seen, no ear has heard, and no mind has imagined what God has prepared for those who love him" (1 Corinthians 2:9, NLT).

I want to give thanks to my family and friends for supporting and believing in me. And lastly, I want to say thank you to all of my future supporters! I pray that this book only does good for the mind, body and soul.

Table of Contents

Introduction

WHO WERE YOU YESTERDAY? is a book of positive quotes and prayers to help you become a newer version of yourself every day!

The only way to become a newer version of yourself is to do something different every day that will improve many areas in your life.

Ask yourself this! Are you tired of tripping over the same rocks? If you answered yes, then it's time for a change! In this book, I will encourage you through a variety of topics to help you start kicking those rocks out of the way so that you can have a clear path to walk on!

What's Holding You Back?

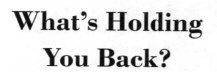

I PRAY AGAINST THE spirits of fear, procrastination, laziness, lack of determination and motivation, lack of self-discipline and self-confidence. Those "spirits" will hinder you from moving forward, people! Hear what I'm saying. I'm speaking from experience and today's time. You wonder why you feel like you should have more going on in your life right now? Why don't you have more? Why aren't you successful and reaching your goals? It all starts with *your* mind-set. How are you thinking? Are you letting your circumstances *limit* you? Break through those limits! You serve a *limitless* God! He is your *ultimate* provider! Don't get discouraged friends. Do what you can do. God will make a way. In reality, you might be limited, but it won't always be that way. It's just for a season. Don't put limits on your thinking. Let your mind-set be optimistic and hopeful. Keep on fighting the good fight of faith! God will *never* fail you!

No matter what you've done in your past, no matter how bad they were or what sins you've committed, God still accepts you for who you are and can still call you to do amazing things in your life. God is a forgiving god. Forget what people say. What God has for you, it is for you! Don't let people remind you what you use to do and how you used to be. Who cares! Are you that person now? Are you still doing those things now? If not, turn the other cheek. If so, today is a new day to give your life over to Christ and start over. Simple! You can't change on your own. Only God can assist you with that. He doesn't want you to do it all alone in your own strength. That's not going to be enough. His strength is sufficient. It is enough!

Are you living a life that pleases God? Or are you doing what is right in your own eyes? God wants us to live a pure life. Ask Him right now to help you live a life that pleases Him.

When dating, show a person how serious you are about your celibate walk, and they will show you how serious they are about you.

Remember that being single is an opportunity for you to learn, grow, and be available for the relationship and man you truly deserve.

Don't get into a relationship out of loneliness. The feeling of loneliness has pushed people into the wrong arms of the wrong person. Being by yourself causes you to have to face yourself. You need to truly learn and embrace who you are and become content.

Being alone does not mean you will be lonely. This time should be spent identifying and exploring your purpose and the things you are passionate about. The process becomes a lot easier when you are working towards something and engaging in activities that truly connect you with what you need and who God created you to be. As a result, you will become more comfortable with yourself and learn to like yourself for who you are.

Ladies, don't get so locked into what you want in a *man* to the point where you overlook the person that's truly best for you because you can't see things clearly. Don't focus so much on what you want. *Needs* are clearly more important than *wants*.

It's so much that goes on in our lives, and we tend to wonder why this is happening to me. As humans, we want to know why, why, why? We want the answers *now*! When you have a relationship with Christ, you're going to be walking "blind." We're never going to know why certain things happen to us, but that's why we have to walk in "faith." Walking in faith is walking blind. God wants to know: Are we going to trust Him even though we can't see what he's doing for us in the background? Just trust that He knows what He's doing. Leave it in His hands.

Look forward to becoming a *better* person. Don't go back to the person you used to be. Change your life for the better. No matter what others say, be who God created you to be. No one is perfect. We've all sinned and made mistakes. Who cares! Don't allow people to bring up your past just to tear you down from becoming a better *you*. Your past does not *define* who *you* are! The choices *you* make now is what will *define* you. Make good choices starting *today*!

This is a new day, a new week. I can't promise you that this week is going to be better than last week but having an optimistic mind-set will help you get through the week much better. Thinking positive, regardless, is always a good start

Sometimes you need that extra push to get things started. Despite of setbacks and closed doors, when you make that decision that you're *not* going to give up until something happens, you've just cranked up determination to *not* quit! No matter how *much* you have to do, no matter how *long* it takes, keep putting forth *effort*! It will *pay off*!

Ladies, get *rid* of that checklist! You will *never* find a perfect man. But you will find an *imperfect* man that will love and cherish *you*!

Being negative *will* screw up *good things* from happening to you. Don't expect good things to happen for you, but then you turn around and start thinking and speaking negative. *Make up your mind!* What do you want *blessings* or *curses*?

That *right* person will see you as *all* that they've *ever* wanted regardless of your flaws! Just being with *you* would mean the *world* to them.

Wouldn't you want the things that you desire the most to happen at the right time? Stand still. Be patient!

We all have flaws and things about us that we need to work on. Nobody is *perfect*! But don't ever change who *you* are just to get someone's attention or approval. Being *yourself* should attract that person to you. You shouldn't have to do anything *extra* to deserve respect or love. If anything, let your inner *beauty* shine. Your mind is more *beautiful* than anything else!

Ladies, I understand that you can become a little disappointed or maybe discouraged because it seems like the "wrong" guys are the *only* ones that seem to find you. Don't feel that way. God has the *right* one just for you! Remember, all of those guys *can't* be with you. Only *one* can. Stay patient and keep the *faith*!

Things *happen* for a reason! Instead of looking at it as God is mad at you or you so-called have "bad luck," look into it a little deeper before you start jumping to conclusions. What is God trying to tell you or reveal to you? There's a lesson in everything that we go through. Stop trying to be the victim all the time! Make some changes, and I guarantee you will get different results. Are you willing to do things differently?

When you think *positive*, things can only get *better*! What are *you* waiting for? Change your *mind-set* today!

No matter *what* has gotten in the way of your dreams, keep that dream *alive*! No matter what you have to do to *make* it happen, *make it happen*!

Only seek approval from *God* and *God* only! If God chose you for a specific purpose, then that means you're *qualified* for it!

Whoever God brings into your life is *only* meant to help you get to where you're heading. But if they leave your life, they were only meant to be in your life for a season!

Everything we experience is *only* to prepare and to strengthen us for what's *ahead*!

You can choose to *think* however you want. But as *long* as you continue to think *negative*, you're leaving an open door for *negativity* to keep coming into your life. Will you choose to change *your* mind-set so you can receive different and *more* positive results in your life?

Be who *God* created you to be. We were *all* made to be *different* and to *stand out*! If God wanted us all to be alike, there wouldn't be *anything* unique about us. He made *us* all different for a *reason*. Be *yourself*! *You* can *only* be *you*! Trying to *follow* the crowd and be somebody else that you're *not,* that shows lack of acceptance to yourself. *Embrace* who *you* are! *Love* the skin you're in. If God loves *you* just the way you *are,* then you need to look in the mirror and love *yourself* too! You are *special*!

It won't always be like this. God's got a plan for *you*! Forget about what happened in the *past.* Don't worry about what's going on in the *now.* Just know that your *future* is looking so much *better*!

You will *not* be defeated! You are an *overcomer*! Your strength comes from the *Lord*! You will *press* your way through *all* obstacles! You will *survive*! You will *make* it!

Trust and believe that God is at *work* for you! He knows your needs and the desires of your heart. Right timing is *everything*!

Regardless of *circumstances* and how you feel, hang on to God's *unchanging* character. Circumstances cannot change the *character* of God. Trust God to keep His promises and remember what God has *already* done for you!

Focus on God, Not Your Circumstances!

THE DEVIL WANTS YOU to put *all* of your energy and time on your issues, problems, and current situations. He wants you to *stress* the heck out of yourself! He's trying to do *anything* to *everything* to try to get you to *quit*! He's trying to do whatever he can for you to *not* pray! He wants you to lose your mind and your faith in God! But guess what, you have the power to decide. Will you *give in* to his mind games, or will you *fight* and gain *strength* through your *faith*? This is *your* life. *Take charge!*

We all will *fall*. What matters is: Are you going to get back up again and keep moving forward?

As long as you're working toward something, something is *bound* to happen. But as long as you're not working toward *anything*, you can't expect for things to *happen*! You can't be *successful* without putting forth *effort*! You *rise* and *fall*. You *rise* and *fall*! It's a *journey*!

God knows what you *need*! He knows what's *good* for you! Trust that He knows what He's doing!

In a relationship, when you have each other, you have all that you *need*. The two of you can *grow* and aim for whatever else you desire *together*! A relationship is *teamwork*, *not* one that is trying to get it all for themselves. It's not just about *you* anymore. It's a "we" thing now.

Don't *quit* because of setbacks! Setbacks are to *strengthen* you to *keep* going! Don't *give up*! Don't *slow down*! Don't *throw in the towel*! Tell yourself *you will make it*! You will *succeed*! *It will happen*! No one can get in the way of *you,* but *you persevere*! *Persevere! You can do this!* Now is the time to prove *you* and *everyone else* wrong!

It's not over yet! God has *your* back. The devil can pull all *types* of strings. But guess what, he doesn't want you to know that he can be defeated by your *faith*! Declare the Word over your circumstances and watch the devil flee in quickness. God will *turn it around*!

Fear draws disaster into every area of your life. It tries to destroy everything you try to do positively with your life. Don't let fear run *your* life.

Lust is a sin. Lust leads to sexual immortality. Lust does *not* come from the Father but from the world.

Take action now! Time waits for *no one*. Tomorrow is not promised. Make changes if you need to. The spirit of procrastination is dangerous. If you keep pushing things back, you will *never* move *forward*. Laziness, fear, lack of self-discipline and confidence can hinder you and slow you down from going to the next level in your life. We're supposed to be moving up in all that we do regardless of setbacks. God wants to promote and elevate us to higher heights. This is the time to not get in the way of God's amazing plan for you.

Yes, God chose you to go through this time in your life to strengthen you and because He knows you will make it through. We all have our own journey to go through to get to where God wants us to be. Stay strong!

20

You come *first*! And *don't* forget that! Self-respect starts with taking care of *you*. Before you make anyone else happy, be happy with *yourself*!

God knows the desires of your heart. Place your heart in His hands, so He can place it in the hands of His best candidate for *you*!

Don't think that God is not preparing you for your soul mate. As much as you desire to be with someone and wonder who he is or where he is or who she is or where she is, they're wondering who and where you are too. They're anticipating on meeting you one day. Pray for your soul mate today!

Speak *change* over your life! Whatever flows from your mouth takes *action*! Speak *life*! Speak *faith*! Speak *positivity*! Take *charge* over *your* life! Make it *happen*!

People, don't you see? The Bible is the ultimate motivational book of *all*! When you read the Word, it gives you confidence in knowing that you will be successful, that you will be *victorious*! God is going to bless you despite of your circumstances. The more you're into the Word, the more positive thoughts and actions you have.

Stay in your lane. Only you can know the *purpose* for your life. This is *not* the time to be trying to *impress* people and be who they want *you* to be!

No one is greater than the other. God has no favoritism. We are all His favorites. So you can *succeed* just like everyone else!

God is the *only* one that can *solve* your problems, give you a *solution,* and *bless* you!

Keep the *faith*! Don't *give up*! *Expect your miracle!*

If you think God has forgotten about you, *He hasn't*! God has great plans for you. Don't let anyone tell you that you can't be *great* because *you are*!

You serve a limitless *God*, but you're limiting what He can do for you when you don't fully *give* yourself over to Him. Let go, and let God! Don't *limit* yourself because of your problems and situations. You are a *child of God*. You are *royalty*. You have a *Father* that can provide for you in *every* area of your life! There is *nothing* that He cannot *do* for you!

Even strong trials cannot blow down a person who is rooted in God!

It's awesome how God knows exactly what we need. He's just waiting for us to ask for it. You say, "Why should we have to ask if He already knows our needs? Why can't He just give it to us?" The reason is because He wants us to rely on Him as our Provider. He wants us to surrender and to put our trust in Him and *only* Him.

If we all had life so *easy* with no complications, receiving blessings wouldn't mean a *thing* to us. But just remember that through your *sufferings* come great *blessings*. God will give you the grace, mercy, and strength to get through *whatever* you may be going through right now.

When you're content with your life knowing that blessings are on its way, it gives you pure *joy* because you know that things are about to change dramatically in a *good* way!

Lessons will always be learned. You *learn*, and you *grow. Move on and do better next time!*

If you're in a rush to be in a relationship, be prepared for some unexpected surprises and disappointments. When you're patient, that means you're trusting that when God sends the one for you, it won't be a mistake. Wouldn't you rather give your heart to the *right* one and try to *avoid* another heartbreak? Or are you just very impatient, desperate and think you're going to die single? Listen, being with someone will not give you *security*! Your confidence is *your* security. If anything, our security comes from God. Philippians 4:19 says, "And my God will supply all your needs according to His riches in glory in Christ Jesus."

Ask yourself this, what's more important, your *heart* or a man?

You know what, I think most people are probably still single because their dream woman or man doesn't exist. The list of things people say they want, they're not going to get everything! A matter of fact, *get rid* of the list or a list altogether. A lot of you all are just plain *picky* and want someone *perfect,* and you're not even perfect yourself. The man or woman you think you want, might not even be good for you *at all!* Some of y'all think y'all know what you *want* but have no clue what you actually *need*. But to those that have decent morals, standards, and desires in a mate and still single, don't worry! God is getting it together!

Be prepared to stay single if you think you're perfect and deserve someone perfect. Keep dreaming.

Ladies, if you're single looking for a mate, don't use your *body* as bait to get a man. Let your *mind* be the bait. If you have to dress half naked with your breast zoomed in all your pictures, booty all sticking out, you're insecure! A guy shouldn't just be attracted to your body. Your physical appearance does *not* define you. If you want someone to respect you, you need to respect *yourself* first. Don't get mad if a guy disrespects you and see's you worthless to date or marry.

The minute you give up, your blessing could be right around the corner. Just hold on. Change is coming! Don't worry about anything!

Stop being *thirsty*! This is for men and women. If they want you, let them show interest and *pursue* you. Being desperate is *not* a good look."

When getting to know someone, you need to have the right motives in the beginning, or you're just starting things off *all wrong*!

God knows you are incapable of being perfect or sinless.

When all you have is God, you have all you need.

Don't waste time on a woman that has *no* self-respect or goals for her life. Find a woman that carries herself with class and that has ambitions and dreams that could benefit her and *you*!

Quitting shows *weakness*! Pressing forward despite of the obstacles, shows true *strength*! Remind yourself why you even started the journey then *stick with it*!

Forget what happened yesterday. God provided you strength for today. Don't worry about tomorrow. God will give you all that you need to make it through your day no matter what your plans are, whether it's school, work, or just plain errands. You're *covered*!

Sacrifices can end up turning into a beautiful thing! Be optimistic!

You pick yourself back up and remind yourself of your *worth*. Do not let *anyone* disrespect you. Just know that those individuals have their own issues, and that they decided to unleash them upon you. Keep it moving!

Today, instead of thinking about your problems and issues, help someone else with their problems and issues. By you helping others, whether it's giving encouraging words, giving a ride, or helping in a financial way can ignite a peace within you to work on your own problems. God focused on helping others 24/7 back in the bible days, why not us? Since when all of the focus is on ourselves? How can we spread the love of God if we make everything me! Me! Me! Do you want to know how God works? This is how: If we take the focus off of us and focus on others like we should, that's how God blesses us in our own struggles and situations.

It's normal to feel uncertain in times of hardship. But knowing that you serve a God that knows your beginning and your ending gives you peace of mind. He knows exactly where you're at in your life right now and He has a solution *just for you*!

You have to step out of your comfort zone in order to step into your destiny. You have to try new things in order to end up in new places. Activate your *faith*! Starve your fears. Faith and fear cannot occupy the same space at the same time. Something has to stay, and something has to leave. Which one will you choose to take up space?

You can't satisfy everybody. No matter how much effort and work you put in, someone is going to say "It's not enough, do more!" Don't overwork yourself for approval and praise. Do what you can and know that you're trying.

Don't get into a relationship if you're already feeling iffy about that person. If you do, it could be a sign to opt out *now* before things go wrong. Trust your instincts. Most of the time, you're *right*!

Nowadays, if you're not living your life a certain way or the "society's" way, they say you're not living life *at all*! Well guess what, I'm not living for anyone but God! Think about it. We were only placed on this earth for a reason, for a *purpose*! We all have a purpose to find out and to fulfill. We all have a customized assignment specially made for each of us. So while you're living your life like everyone else's, you're actually the one that's wasting time. Live life with *purpose*!

Why stress over things that *you know* you have no control over *at all?* When you're constantly stressing, worrying, doubting, you're actually making your situation worse than what it already is. By you doing all of that, is that helping you in any kind of way? If not, why do it? Try a new strategy! Take on a new approach! You need to relax and take a deep breath. Clear your thoughts from *all* negativity. Figure out what you *can* do in that situation, and then *do just that!* Other than that, pray and leave it in God's hands. He has the power to change your situation, *not you!* Don't try to face the world all by yourself because you're not equipped for that. We are to rely on God for *everything!* So today, if you are facing hardships and challenges, take them on in a more positive way. Your situation may not change immediately, but how you handle them in the meantime will build up perseverance to get through them. *Trouble* won't last *always!*

People will judge you *regardless!* It comes to show their maturity if they can't just first get to know you without making conclusions right off the back about you. Make sure you stay 100 percent with yourself. Trust me. A lot of people don't even deserve the opportunity to get to know you if they "supposedly" have a negative vibe toward you already. *You are destined for greatness! You are who God created you to be.* The opinions of man are irrelevant when God says *you're everything* to Him.

Letting go of the stresses of life, giving them to God gives room to have hope, to smile, and to relax. Though this world is full of ups and downs, it's always best to smile from the inside out. Smile for a better future! Things won't always be the same. Seasons are always changing. Things will get better! Do you believe that?

Leave the physical stuff to the side, and love the beauty that's within that person. That beauty is what lasts a lifetime!

Don't do anything that you don't want to do. Don't settle. Don't allow things to be done to you that you don't agree with or like or support at all. Don't let anyone or anything pressure you to feel like that's all there is, so you just go with the flow and accept it like that's as good as it gets. You deserve what you desire, *no less*! Some people may not understand your decision, but it's not meant for them too. It's your life! What matters to you won't matter to them. Friendships and relationships might crumble and fall, but hey, life goes on. It's not easy making decisions, but *you* deserve to be *happy*!

If you don't love yourself first, how do you expect to love someone else? Find yourself, appreciate yourself, and love yourself. You come *first*!

When you wait for something real, you know your worth and will not tolerate for second best but for God's best.

When you settle, be ready to accept all that comes with it! Good and bad.

There's only one *you*. Why change and become someone else if God created you to be different and to *stand out*?

Be yourself! Stay 100 percent. Everybody can't hang with you. Only those that are meant to be in your life will stay. People come and go. *That's life*!

Make sure you're the right person for them. You're single in this season for a reason which means this is the time to work on and better yourself in every area of your life. Don't think you got it all together and that you don't need to work on anything because we are all a work in progress. Pray and ask God to reveal any hidden things about you that you need to improve on. If you're still damaged from a past relationship, ask God to heal you and to stitch your heart back together. He will do *just* that.

No one will respect you unless you show confidence in who you are. Accept and embrace everything about you then others will do the same. It all starts with you.

Never alter who you are just to accommodate what somebody else wants from you. It's no one's job to try to change anyone. They either accept you for you or move on. We're placed on this earth to be who God created us to be, not who man wants us to be.

Make decisions that are going to bring out positive outcomes.

Best thing to do is to sit back, relax, and let God take over your current situations.

A temporary moment is not worth a permanent soul exchange. Wait on God and on the right person that's going to make the wait worth it.

Ladies, forget the materialistic things. Be a real backbone. There's *nothing* wrong with enjoying life, but what really matters is appreciating the person and letting them know that you *support* them. A guy would really see *your* worth if they know that you're going to be with them through thick or thin, rain or shine, ups and downs, light and dark moments they may have. If you can walk through the fire with them, they will know that you'll walk through *anything* with them. Guys just want to know if you'll *always* be there and *not* run out on them once something bad happens. *Be loyal* ladies!

Are you familiar with the saying "Good things come to those that wait"? That is *actually* true in a sense. Waiting for something *patiently* is always a good thing. So when it comes to relationships, wouldn't you want your next relationship to be a *good* one? Develop *self-control* so you can develop patience. Rushing to have someone won't bring a *healthy* relationship to the table.

Having patience will *always* calm your anxious heart!

You need to desire God's heart first before you desire *anything* else!

People crave sex *not* because it feels good and it's enjoyable. It's because deep down inside, they want *love*! They're just looking for it in the *wrong* way with the *wrong* people. They don't want to just have sex with someone that's attractive and call it a day. And if you do have sex for that reason, you're in *denial*! Why do you think they call it a "soul tie"? You're at home still reminiscing on everybody that you did it with. You still have feelings for some of them. Sex is *real*! It gets deep down into your subconscious and spirit. Sex is a beautiful thing between a husband and wife, but it's *dangerous* when you're *not* married. Emotions run deep, and it gets to you no matter how strong you think you are. Once you've gotten too deep into the spirit of fornication, God is your *only* way out!

Waiting till marriage probably sounds like a long way to go when you think about celibacy. But the benefits are *worth* it. If it seems complicated or difficult for you to do, don't do it for yourself then. Do it for God! Do it because it's the *right* thing to do. He will give you the strength to fight temptation and to stick to your celibacy walk. He's *not* going to ask you to do something that He won't help you get through. He's *not* like that! He will provide assistance with whatever you need. Think about it! How would your mate feel that you don't need sex from them just to show physical love and appreciation and that you rather do it the *right* way? Do you know how special a person would feel the fact that you were celibate for them and wanted to wait for something and someone *real*? That's *love*!

We should *never* think that we cannot be used for *Your* glory. God reveals to us our *purpose*, and let us start to immediately operate in it. We are *special*, and we were created for *your* good works. We will complete Your work that You have assigned to us.

You say you deserve *better*, but your actions are saying something else. You're going around hunting for the *right* one when you need to be content being single first so you can choose better mates. Being desperate and thirsty, you're going to overlook the *right* one and fall for the *wrong* one. While you're single, build a relationship with God so He can prompt you when the *right* one has arrived. God communicates in different ways, but you have to give Him 100 percent of your attention so He can give you direction like when to move forward and when to *not* make a move with that person.

You were *chosen* for greatness! You were placed on this earth with a special assignment. You have a *purpose*! God has equipped you to do whatever He needs you to do. All that you *need*, you already possess it inside of you. Go for it! Now is *your* time to get ahead!

When you do things God's way, you can *never* go wrong! God will *never* lead you astray or off course. His way is *perfect*!

Having closed doors or doors being closed in your life is *not* a good feeling at first. But what a *relief* it is to know that you don't have to get into *something* that you weren't meant to get into. One less headache!

God looks out for us even when we don't understand what's going on!

Some people look at God as if He's a genie or something. He doesn't grant wishes! He answers prayers. God blesses you because He loves you, cares about you, and you deserve those blessings. He is *your* master. You are *not* His master! You're obviously praying to God because you need His help and assistance which means you admit that all power are in His hands. You're coming to Him because you're relying and depending on Him. So don't get it twisted. You are on His watch. He is *not* on yours! You are going to Him for help, so that means you need to have patience.

What are your motives when you need God for something?

Trust me, God knows the *desires* of *your* heart. He wants to bless you with those things. But He wants you to *want* Him more than those things. Let Him know that He's *first* in *your* life. He doesn't want you to *always* be thinking about everything else except Him.

Spending time with God is a great way to clear out the clutter that's trashing up *your* life. Clutter as in *distractions*, people that don't *belong* in your life, *negative* thoughts, etc., you name it! Get rid of it! Clutter are *hindrances*! You say you can't hear from God, but He *communicates* through His Word. You have to be in the Word! You need to do a summer cleanup and *get rid* of things or maybe *people* that are blocking *your* blessings from coming through. How can you hear from God if your mind is *always* on everything else? Will you listen to the *noise* of the world, or will you listen to God's *soft* voice so He can lead and guide you?

You have to make changes to get results. Time waits for no man. It's time to reap *your* blessings. So start cleaning up!

You may *not* like where you are in *your* life right now, but just the fact that you know that God is *about* to take you places, just the fact that you are on this earth for a *purpose* whether you are already operating in your purpose or not should give you *peace* knowing that God has special plans laid out for you. And with *obedience*, those plans will bring *great* blessings to your life.

God has equipped you to survive whatever storms you are *facing* right now! You just have to *believe* that you possess those things inside of you!

We shouldn't judge people by how they look or dress and think that they're not struggling with some issues or have gone through anything in life. We tend to make things look like we have it all together on the outside, but we're battling storms on the inside. We don't have to tell and show the world that our life is falling apart. You'll be surprised at some stories people could tell you if you just ask!

You need to stop trying to control *your* life, and let God take control of the wheel. He's the *only* one that knows where you're heading in life, you *don't*! By you trying to find *your* own way and all, that's how you cause *yourself* to run into dead ends and roadside ditches because you *won't* let God lead you. God holds the map to *your* destiny, *not* you.

We've *all* gone through *a lot* in our lives whether it has to do with family issues, friends, school, work, financial struggles, marriages, or relationships. Nobody knows what we've gone *through* or is actually going through right now unless we tell it or show it. It's sad when *people* start to see others get *blessed*, and they have a *negative* attitude toward them as if they don't deserve it. God knows our *history*, and He blesses *us* because we kept our *faith* and continued to *trust* in Him that He will bring us through whatever we're going through.

Being *single* is *not* a curse! Embrace *your* single-ness! This is the time to just *focus* on you! Eliminate all *distractions*!

Stay plugged into the Source (the Word of God). You don't have to worry about power outages. God is "not" FPL. God is an everlasting, cordless generator *full* of power. The only way to be disconnected from God (the Source) is when you're being disobedient or just plainly blocking Him out of your life. If you need to talk to God, you don't have to be placed on hold. You don't have to take a ticket and wait in line. God is available 24/7, 365 days year-round. God comes to where *you* are. Isn't that convenient? Now that's awesome treatment right there. It can't get no better than that.

Do you want to know who the best person you could be like? *Yourself!* Want to know why? Because no one else can be like you but *you*! People are walking around here trying to be someone that they're *not*! If you were supposed to be like everyone else, it wouldn't be a *struggle* or *confusing*, right? Be yourself and accept your *true* identity. If you don't know who you are, ask God to reveal to you who He created you to be. God gave you your own *unique* set of fingerprints for a reason. You cannot be duplicated! Why try to be an *imitation* when you were made as an *original*? He took precious time creating you to be *different* than everyone else. Stop trying to blend in when you were born to *stand out*!

The wise never has to say much. Their actions speak for them.

God's timing is *always* the best timing. Whatever He does *will* turn out *right*! If you trust in Him, you should not worry about if everything is going to be okay. Just know that it *will*!

Trust that, wherever you are in *your* life right now, it *will* get better. It's all a part of the plan!

Your *past* does not define you! What you do *now* does. So who cares what people say about who you *used* to be or what you *used* to do. God has already *forgiven* you! So ask *yourself*, who are they to *judge* if the God you serve has the *final* say?

Trust in Him. Rely on Him. Wait on Him. Believe in Him. Rejoice in Him, and relax in Him. Everything *will* come through! Don't give up! Your *blessing* could be right around the corner!

Do you notice that most of the time you're thinking negative and wonder why your life is the way it is now? Check your *attitude*! You're probably the *one* that's causing your life to be how it is. Before change can come, change *your* thinking. You have to make the first change!

Make sure whoever you get with has a *real* relationship with God! The foundation of a relationship needs to be God. If *not*, you're in an imbalanced relationship already. If he doesn't know God, he won't know how to love, lead, or have the right relationship with you!

As soon as you wake up, the devil tries to have you wake up thinking about your problems and issues. You have to beat him to it and start telling *yourself* that God is in *control*! That things *will* get better no matter how long it takes. If a negative thought comes to your mind, you need to quickly think and speak *positive* to yourself. We've all woken up to those kinds of thoughts. But that's how your day starts off all *wrong* because you're waking up *stressing*! God says He will keep you perfect whose mind is stayed on Him. So keep your mind on *Him*!

Surround *yourself* with people that are going where you're going. Although, everyone can't go where you're going. Be around encouraging, motivated, positive, determined, successful people. Be around people that will give *constructive* criticism, not *destructive* criticism. They should help you get to the top, *not* make everything a *competition*. Who you *surround* yourself with is who you end up *becoming*! Check your circle!

Every day when you wake up, *always* remind yourself where you're heading. Despite of how you may wake up and feel, *you* need to make sure that whatever you do *today* is going to benefit you *tomorrow*. Whatever you do *every day* needs to be things that will help you have a *better* future. Stick to your current plan! Laziness will *hinder* your progress!

While you're ripping and running, going to work or school or whatever you may be involved in, don't forget to treat yourself and have fun. Life can be *stressful* but learn how to laugh and enjoy life as well. Regardless of your circumstances, life doesn't have to be *serious* all time. Laugh through your *struggles* because your situations won't last long anyway, so enjoy every moment of *your* life! Always give *yourself* credit for all that you've done and *reward* yourself.

There are times when things are just *falling* apart in your life. What a *horrible* situation that can be. All you feel you can do at the moment is find a *solution*. In times like that, stressing over multiple things will *not* help the situation get better. Knowing God's Word will give you peace in the midst of controversy and turmoil. The Bible is filled with instructions designed to help you live a successful, peaceful life.

You have to understand that things don't happen *fast*. Whatever it is that you *want*, it takes time! Don't rush things, and then it ends up *not* working out because of impatience. There is a process with *everything* that we go through. Just *trust* God's timing. When the time is *right*, everything will fall into position.

Crave for someone's mind. Crave for someone's heart. Love a person *not* based on the physical only. Lust gets in the way of developing true feelings for someone!

The *one* that's for you might *not* have all the qualities that you want in a lover. But if they are willing to be with you forever, flaws and all, *nothing* else should matter. At the end of it all, their *love* will remain out of *all* things!

No matter what you may be going *through*. I don't care what it is. Don't let God be your *last* option. Don't make God your last "go-to" person. Why *not* go to the *One* that has all the answers? The *One* that can work *everything* out for you. The *One* that understands what's going on in your life. The *One* that can change your *circumstances* at any time! Why waste time with people that are *limited* to what they can do for you? God is *unlimited*! Nothing is *too* hard for God! Go to the *Source* for assistance and relief!

Don't seek God just because you need *help*. Seek God because you want a real, intimate relationship with Him. Seek Him because you want to live that life *full* of blessings. Think about it. How would you feel if somebody *only* came to you for help and then once they got it, that's it? Then they don't need you *anymore*! Wouldn't you feel used and unappreciated? Imagine God feeling that way when you do that to Him. He wants it to be something *real* between you two. God doesn't bless you because you ask for it. He blesses you because He hopes one day you'll invite Him into your life!

54

In order to be successful or *get* to success, you have to know how it feels to start from the *bottom*. You have to know how it feels to be *stressed* out and *exhausted*. You have to know how it feels to *not* have support or *help* at all. You have to know how it feels to have *closed* doors. You have to know how it feels when people don't want to give you a *chance*! Success is *not* easy nor is it free! It comes with a *price*! How much are *you* willing to pay?

What you are going through right now is paving the way to *your* breakthrough! God knows *all* of the hard work that you've been doing. He will *reward* you because *you* deserve it!

You might *not* like where you are in *your* life right now. But until God opens up doors for you, you're just going to have to *accept* where you are at the *moment* and *do* what you got to do. The key to receiving blessings is to show faith, patience, contentment, and gratefulness. Work with what you got!

Why get *mad* over situations that you have *no* control over? Like is it *worth* ruining your day? Put your *trust* in God! Attitude is *everything*. So check *yours*!

Those things that you want so *bad*, are you willing to work as *hard* as you need to, to have those things? Don't say you want it but don't have the *motivaton* nor the *determination* to get it. Life doesn't come to you on a silver platter. You *work* for what *you* want. There's no such thing as "microwave" success!

Some of us are waiting for things to just happen for us. Taking *action* plays a major role in *making* things *happen*! If there's no movement, then there's no progress! Do your part!

If you can't learn how to be happy *alone*, what makes you think when you get a girlfriend or boyfriend that they're going to bring you happiness? The couples you see walking around smiling, holding hands, hugging, and kissing doesn't mean a thing! You don't know what's going on behind *closed* doors away from the public eye. Learn how to love *yourself* first.

Take each day a step at a time. Keep a steady pace. Don't speed up or slow down. Stay focused on what you can do in the now, and God will make a way for everything else. Cast all of your cares on Him. It's *only* so much that we can do, so why *not* let God take care of what we have no power to change? We serve a *big* God!

God knows what you *need*. He's just waiting for you to ask Him. Some people think they can take care of themselves, and that they don't need God. But when you let go of all that pride, ego, and so-called "independence" and surrender yourself to Christ, letting Him know that you need His help and that you can't do it alone, that's when God steps in to *take action*!

Did you know that when you start to worry, doubt, think or speak negative, have fear, be disobedient when God tells you to do something, become lazy and procrastinate, that's how you miss out on *your* blessings? You sit here and pray to God about your needs and the desires of *your* hearts, but you don't have the faith to back it up.

It's sad how people feel that they should bring up your past faults and mistakes just because you *chose* to live a better yet "godly" life. They only do that because they're not happy with their lives and feel that the only way to deal with their unhappiness is to pull other people down with them. I said this before, and I'll say this again. Your *past* does *not* define who you are. What you do *now* is what defines you. Your past should be your *best friend*, not your enemy. Want to know why? Because your past should be the reason why you are the person you are *today*! Through all the mess, issues, problems, and circumstances that has happened in your life back then, it has molded and shaped you into the person that you are right now! Don't let people feel like they can *control* you with their destructive words of criticism and judgment. Be *strong* in your pursuit, and *don't* change who you are for *anyone*!

Every new day is a blessing from God to let us know that He's not finished with us *yet*!

Be with someone that sees you the same way that you see them. Make sure you two are in agreement and have a clear understanding about how you feel toward each other. You can't *force* love. It's either there or not.

Get all the facts before you make a decision. Never jump to conclusions too early. Things just might switch up on you! Give it some time to play out!

Distractions come in different ways, shapes, and forms. They are meant to steer you *off* your course. Get rid of *distractions*! Stay focused on what's ahead!

When you rush things, that's when things get *overlooked*. God wasn't in a rush to send you that person so when He does, He expects you to have that same *patience* and to take your time getting to know the *one* that He has sent for you. Taking your time should *never* be an issue. It's the *safest* route to go. Really getting to know that person, you'll *discover* a whole lot and won't have to worry about unexpected surprises. Even though things do *pop* up, the important things will *reveal* itself in due time.

Patience plays an important role when it comes to blessings. Don't become impatient and screw things up for yourself. Self-discipline is *strongly* advised!

When others see you as a *nobody*, God sees you as a *somebody*. You were made in His image. So when it's time to be promoted and elevated, it'll happen for you and *not* for them. Watch your attitude toward other people because you just might ruin your own blessings. Remember, "God looks at your heart *not* your physical appearance or how successful you may be."

We all have gone through good or bad situations in our lives. They are called experiences. Experiences *only* turn into wisdom if you have learned something from them. Once you have that wisdom, it's always good to share it with someone in need.

If you can't *follow* Christ, how can you *lead* others?

It's easy to stand with a crowd; it takes courage to stand alone.

We *only* made it through because we kept the *faith* and *believed* that we *were* going to make it through. Continue to have the mind-set that no matter what, *stay positive*!

Why dream when you are the *only* one who can make your dreams come *true*?

If yesterday wasn't so good for you, do something different so you can enjoy *today*! Don't bring yesterday's drama into a brand-new day that God has blessed you with. Today is another chance to get different results. But it all starts with you! Will you let today be a rerun of yesterday?

A lot of people don't know who they are because they're *too* busy trying to be somebody that they're *not*! Ask God to reveal to you *who* you really are, and from then on, *be yourself!*

You don't need to *worry* about how God is going to get your needs met. Just know that *He* will meet your needs.

Despite of what you may be going through right now, celebrate in advance for your breakthrough is near!

Your time is coming! God is still preparing *everything* for you. But you do need to prepare and position yourself for your *blessings*!

God knows the plans that He has for us. We don't know what the future holds. So by having *closed* doors, that's how He can get us to move *forward* and in the right direction. Don't think closed doors lead to a *dead end* and think that's it. A blessing is *always* around the corner!

If God blessed you with someone that you could be in a relationship with, that person should *only* bring you into an even deeper relationship with God. If that relationship is making you distant from God, get your priorities together. God should *always* be number one!

When you know *your* worth, you would know that you deserve *better*! Don't subtract anything about you for someone else. You should *only* be an addition to that person's life!

If a guy wants to pursue you, as women, we have a role to play as well. The guy doesn't necessarily have to do all the work. It's fifty-fifty in everything! So I'm not saying the guy has to chase the girl, or the girl has to chase the guy either. Men don't have time for games just as much as we don't. If you're interested in someone, *show it*! If not, be *real*, and let them know!

If a guy is really interested in you, other women wouldn't confuse him to continue pursuing *just you*! Yes, guys have options, but it would be something about you that stands out amongst the rest!

Men will come and *go*! But the *one* for you will come and *stay*! Being with you will be His new home.

If it's meant to happen, it will happen *regardless*, no matter *what*! You just need to keep your focus on God and be open to new love! Forget the past. This is *now*!

Your *dream* life is *not* as far away as you think! With sweat and tears, once you get there, you'll be glad that you *never* gave up! It's awesome when you can look back at the journey. You coming from the bottom and rose to the top despite of negativity, obstacles, and length of time. Just *imagine*!

Take charge, and *do* what you know is *right*, no matter how *hard* it may be because *nothing* in life is easy. Even if *no one* understands why you're doing it, which means *no* support system! Everyone *won't* understand, and that's fine because they're *not* the ones feeling strongly about it, *you are*! You might as well *not* explain yourself to people. Just do it for you and for you *only*!

Be ready for what God has in stored for you!

Only looking forward! *Never* looking back!

This year will be the year that *you will* be able to do the things you've always wanted to do! I don't care what happened years ago that has slowed you down or even stopped you. This *year* you will be *limitless*!

Quitting is easy but has *no* results. Hard work isn't easy, but it comes with *satisfying* results!

As long as you do your part, God will make sure it *happens*!

Change can be a *beautiful* thing! Embrace it when it comes! Time to experience something *new*!

Stop thinking about how long something is going take to happen! Just *focus* on getting there. *That's it*!

How *bad* do you want it? Are you willing to go the distance? Will you make the sacrifice?

Just because you have *goals* but don't know how to reach them, doesn't mean it's *impossible*!

We all have a *purpose* for our lives. It's up to us to *discover* it and to *fulfill* it!

When you're getting the *results* that you want, you'll try to *avoid* messing up what you've already accomplished by any means necessary!

As long as you're *working* towards something, something is bound to happen! You must take *action* to get a *reaction*!

Sometimes we need to have some *quiet* time alone so that we can have a *clear* mind. Great ideas can't get through *clutter*!

Enjoy *life*! Whether it goes your way or not, find happiness in everything! Living life includes good times and bad times. But *never* lose your *joy*!

People *will always* try to give you advice. Take the *good* out of it and leave the *bad* behind. All advice is *not* helpful!

Why stress about your problems when God has fixed *bigger* and *greater* problems than yours? Can He not fix your problems as well? Some of you are expecting that *instant* rescue *all the time* when sometimes things take time to come together. Just because it may take a while doesn't mean it's not going to happen. We *all* need *patience* and *faith*! Why don't you pray and ask God to give those things so that *waiting* won't be such a *struggle* for you!

72

You can do whatever you put your mind to do! You just can't *give up* when things get a bit difficult!

Don't let your troubles weigh you down. Trouble don't last always! Fast forward into the future and imagine yourself without those troubles. Because guess what? It will soon be reality only if you believe!

Focus on what you can *do* something about, *not* on what is *out* of your control!

You may not know what to do about the situation that you're in right now, but the best things to do is to pray and keep making moves!

Never stop *praying*!

Never stop taking *action*!

Be grateful for what you have right now because eventually you'll have more!

All you need to do is have a plan and stick with it! That's when you will start seeing *results*!

Get *excited*! There's so many opportunities coming your way this year! Do you believe that?

If you stay positive and patient, waiting for good things to happen for you wouldn't be so difficult.

Just because you haven't done something before doesn't mean you can't do it! Try it and see what happens! You won't know unless you give it a chance!

It doesn't matter what situation you're in. If God brought you through a situation before, He'll definitely do it again and again! He is *not* a one-time God! So instead of allowing your situation to take over your emotions today, put a smile on your face, and know that God already worked your whole, entire situation out. You just can't see it yet, but you will, eventually. Stay positive my friends!

Life struggles are temporary! They may slow you down, but don't let them stop you!

I believe that *better* is coming!

What I see now is *not* forever!

Don't lose your faith!

Don't lose your focus!

Don't allow the enemy to try to remove you where God has you established at.

God's purpose will bring you to your future! Your future will be *greater* than your purpose!

Learn to be humble and ask God to help you when you really don't know what else to do. Stop trying to figure everything out on your own, creating more stress for yourself. It doesn't mean that you're weak because you're in need of help. You're accepting the fact that in life, you will always need help with something. It's totally okay!

Just remember as each day goes by, you're getting closer to your goal! That's why it's very important to keep moving forward! Focus on your future, *not* on your past. Your future holds change and brand-new opportunities! If anything, don't repeat past mistakes! Learn from them and *do better*! You got this! No one can hold you back but *yourself*!

Stay motivated and determined my friends! The year has only just begun! Your hard work will *not* be a waste! Something has to happen when you are persistent! This is the year when you *only* accept positivity into your life. Whomever is *not* on board with your dreams and goals, kindly drop them off at the next bus stop!

In life, you won't always get all the answers right then and there. You can't always take the safe road. At some point, you will have to take risks! It can be scary at first, but you won't know what "could" happen unless you do. Why miss out when life is already too short? Taking risks is taking a leap of faith!

If I strive to *do* better, I will *be* better! Change cannot happen unless I am willing to sacrifice some things in my life! Change is a good thing because you're allowing yourself to grow!

If God has blessed you so much last year that you think you've seen it all, I've got news for you! Just wait and see. This year, the *best* is yet to come!

If you never make mistakes, how will you learn? If everything always goes right, how would you know how to be strong during bad times? Good and bad things happen for a reason! There's a lesson *always* to be learned in everything! Take advantage of every experience! Growth is a part of life!

Make this year *count*! Whatever didn't happen for you last year, have *hope and confidence* in it for this year! Continue where you left off! Keep going! You have a whole brand-new year in front of you!

Don't worry about other people's accomplishments. Be happy for them, and then focus on your goals! When you don't have goals to focus on, that's how depression and jealousy starts to sneak in.

When you're happy when *great* things happen for others, *great* things will happen for you too!

If you keep sowing and/or planting small amounts of effort towards your future, you will reap a harvest! Whatever you do now *will* affect your future! Whatever you do now does *matter*!

If you don't work towards what you want, it'll always be just a dream.

Don't get mad at God when things are *not* going your way. Instead, *trust* Him!

When you don't quit and give up, you're giving a chance for good things to happen for you! You're allowing a way for them to get through to you!

Want to see how *faith* works? Trust God when you don't know what else to do!

If you are going through a lot right now, once you put a prayer request in to the Lord, just know *change* is coming!

Here's a metaphor! You are at a restaurant. You're feeling hungry, and your stomach hurts. How you're feeling at the moment is temporary because you know you put in a food order which means your food is on its way. Just to add, where I'm getting at is, don't revolve around temporary issues. Things that won't last forever shouldn't have so much control over you.

God, You are in control!
This day is in Your hands!
I will make the *best* of it!

Take your concerns to God before you try to make decisions on your own. We can easily make decisions based off of our emotions. Clear your head then pray!

What you do now will determine how your future will be. You have to make good decisions so that your future can be set! It will be worth it in the end!

If you're in a relationship or a marriage, *always* keep God first and *always* work towards bettering your-selves and each other!

No matter how *simple* your life may seem, God has much *bigger* plans in store for you!

If you have a goal, you need to set a date for when you want to accomplish that goal. You need to have something to look forward to when it gets closer to that time.

As long as we live, we will have tests and trials. But do you really want negativity to always take over so that you can have that "victim" mind-set and feel as if the world is against you? Do your problems really have that much power over you? There is *always* hope! There is *always* another way! Stop accepting what life allows to happen as the end! It's *not* the end! God has the *final* say! Now what problems do you have that's *impossible* for God to turn around? *None! There's nothing my God cannot do!*

As soon as you want to complain, count your blessings. You'll be amazed!

I am *not* going to settle for *less* for anything! *I will* enjoy *every* area of my life!

Don't wait for a feeling to come to motivate you! You need to be capable of motivating yourself whether the feeling is there or not!

It doesn't matter when your blessing comes or what kind of blessing it is. Just already have a grateful heart!

Get ready for a new beginning! Another *year*, new *opportunities*! Leave your mistakes, failures, breakups, divorces, missed opportunities, fake friends, negative medical reports, lost car, lost job, lost home, etc., in last year! This year has *no* room for the past! So start cleaning up your mind and your life *now*! You can only move *forward*!

Don't be *discouraged* if some things don't go through or happen the way you planned. God has something way *better* than what you had in mind!

I don't care what happens throughout my day today! I have the power to enjoy it regardless! I will *not* allow people or things to sway my emotions!

Stop asking God for a sign. Just *trust* Him!

Just because you're stuck in a situation doesn't mean to not do anything. That's how we make no progress whatsoever. Pray, make a decision, then act on it!

I don't want to live my life without a purpose. I want to enjoy life knowing that I am doing exactly what I was destined to do!

While you're waiting on God to send you that special person, don't waste time! Since none of us are perfect, work on any areas in your life that need some maintenance done. So when God does say it's time, you'll be better than before.

Working on yourself doesn't mean you're necessarily changing who you are entirely. You are working on areas that could cause setbacks for you!

If I quit, I'll *never* succeed. If I quit, I'll *never* know how much potential I truly have. If I quit, the *only* person that would be living their life less than the best would be *me*! That's *not* who God created me to be. If He says I can make it and that I'm more than a conqueror, then I need to *believe* what He says. Steps of *faith* will make things a reality.

When you need God to come through for you, that's when you gotta put *all* of your *faith* in and *believe* that a *blessing* will come out of it! It's like as if you're gambling or betting *all* of the money that you've have, taking a *risk* hoping that you'll get a *big* win!

When you're waiting for your prayers to be answered, make sure that you've done *your part*. Sometimes we can be waiting for God to make something happen when He's actually waiting on us to put some *effort* in and to speak *faith* on our situation. So what are you waiting for? *Take action and stay prayerful!*

Don't let things or people get to you. It's only a test!

It doesn't matter how many times you make a mistake. What matters is trying to *overcome* whatever that's keeping you from moving forward! Your *determination* will get you through it! You can't throw in the towel because you didn't get it right the first couple of times. Whether you quit now or later, it still won't make a difference. Do what you have to do in order to get by!

Just *expect* things to get better! It doesn't matter when it happens. Just have that attitude and mind-set!

Forget about the past, focus on the present, plan for the future!

Change happens when you've had enough of the *same*!

There is *no* need to be conceited. Just *love* yourself enough to know your *worth*!

No matter what the devil tries to plot on you, God has a plan!

I'm just a cracked pot God is using to let His light shine through!

I will *not* accept anything less than God's best!

I will *not* limit myself based off of where I am in my life, the words I speak, nor my actions!

I rather lose who I am to God than to the world. So if I seem different, it's because God changed me, *not* the world!

Just be grateful to be *alive*! As long as you live, strive to be *better* and to do *better*! *Never* stop because of limitations! There's *always* a way to get to where you're trying to go! *Allow* hardships to turn into times of *strength* and allow them to help you *grow*!

If God didn't allow us to go through hardships, we wouldn't have a need to have faith. And if we didn't need to have faith, we wouldn't be able to please God!

If you're in such a rush for a certain thing to happen, you could miss small important details that could really benefit you along the way. *Take it slow but stay persistent!*

It's never too late to start over. Just don't give up and *quit*!

Don't wait to be excited when you have reached your goal! Be excited through the process!

If you don't sacrifice for what you want, then you really don't want it that bad! No one is successful without having to *sacrifice* something!

Strengthen yourself mentally, emotionally, and spiritually so you won't fall apart during *tough* times!

Don't forget about your past completely! Learn from it and apply it to your future!

Don't *envy* what other people have! Work for what you want! Jealousy will get you *nowhere*!

If you put your *trust* in people, you are *only* setting yourself up for disappointment. Instead, put your *trust* in God. He will *never* fall short from keeping His word. He doesn't *break* promises!

When you pray, instead of complaining about what's going wrong in your life, switch it up! Start *thanking* Him for what you *do* have and also letting Him know what you are *believing* in Him to do for you. He wants to see your *gratefulness* and your *confidence* towards Him!

If God has a plan for your life, *no one* can stop it, not *family, friends, enemies, finances, not* even *you*! It will come to pass *regardless*!

Just because you're close to reaching your goals doesn't mean to slow down! Stay at the pace you started with until the end!

When you have sinned or slipped up, allow God to:

- Forgive you
- Instruct you
- Give you His wisdom

If we are in a situation, God will either get us *out* or *through* it! Either way, we're coming out! God wouldn't allow us to go through a situation that we cannot handle! He is *always* with us!

You can't expect different results when you keep doing the same things over and over again!

With God, I can do *anything* and will get through *everything*!

When God is your biggest supporter, your support system is *set*!

Praise God regardless of what you're going through!

If you don't doubt God but instead trust Him, He will help you!

The power of staying positive during difficult times helps you to remain focused on your goals! Don't lose sight of where you're headed just because of temporary obstacles!

Whatever state I find myself in, I learned how to be secure, knowing that God will supply all my needs. He'll work things out for my good!

It will get better. God is in control!

Refuse to *settle* for less!

Go after *bigger* and *better* things!

Be excited before the blessing comes! Don't let anyone or anything steal your joy! Get ready for things to turn around for your good!

It doesn't matter where you are in your life right now, what you don't have, or what you see happening around you. Still go after that dream or goal that you have. Quitters *never* win, and winners *never* quit!

God wouldn't hold back blessings, *especially* if you've been faithful! He wants to give you the *desires* of your heart. Only *you* can interfere with that even happening. So make sure that you're not getting in your own way!

If you're trying to clear your mind so that you can think straight, start by eliminating distractions (which could be a person/people or things) and negative thoughts!

Don't get discouraged because things are taking a little longer than expected. The race is still worth it.

I just want to live a purpose-filled life! Doing things that have meaning, things that will make a positive impact on someone!

No matter what, *expect* the best out of every situation. Things could turn around at any time! What can you lose by just being positive?

Do what you believe in and forget about other people's opinions! Everyone won't always understand!

If you don't like a situation that you're in, *do something about it*! People that complain are mainly the ones that are *not* trying to do anything about their problems. If *you are* doing something about them, then *stop* complaining!

When you *discover* yourself, you'll know what you *deserve* to have!

If you can change your thinking, God can change your life.

God's favor surrounds you like a shield. It doesn't matter what the circumstances look like in your life. Regardless of how many people tell you it can't be done, if you persevere, declaring the favor of the Lord and having an attitude of faith, God will open doors for you and change your circumstances on your behalf.

If you want *change*, then you'll do anything to get it!

If your plan doesn't work out, God already had a *better* plan that will work out! Just ask Him what He has in store for you, and He'll reveal it to you in due time.

If God blesses you with a brand-new day, it doesn't matter how many mistakes you've made in your past or yesterday. You have a chance to *change*, to be *different*, and to do *better*!

I *strongly* believe that you should be around individuals that will *accept* you for *who* you are, instead of individuals that don't or won't *ever* understand you. They will *only* try to *change* you! Your *identity* is all you have! Don't lose what defines *you*!

I can *only* go but *up* if I keep pressing on!

My goal is to complete whatever assignment God has on my life! I'm *not* worrying about anybody or anything right now. I have a *purpose*. I have a *destiny*! And I will fulfill it!

Remember, you can be in whatever mood you choose to be in, no matter what people say or do. You have that control!

Even if you don't see anything yet, God is *still* working on something behind the scenes!

Seek to have *more* of God and *less* of everything else!

You can't be *where* you want to be unless you *do* what you have to do in order to get there!

Don't wait for people to acknowledge and appreciate the things that you do for them. God acknowledges and appreciates *everything* that you do, and you will be blessed for doing so.

When you *move*, God *moves*!

If you keep praying, something is bound to happen!

I'm just *expecting* amazing things to happen for me. I'm *not* dwelling on past mistakes, failures, disappointments, and setbacks. I can't go back to the past to change anything. I can *only* make sure that with each *new* day that comes, that I put those twenty-four hours to good use!

No matter what, I'm going *be* better and *do* better! I am going to *purposely* surprise myself and *show* myself how much *potential* I really have.

I'm *not* going to wait until God blesses me to give Him praise. I'm going to praise Him from the beginning to the end of it all.

When things start to get complicated and difficult, that doesn't mean to *quit* and run away. Life is *full* of ups and downs. The *only* way to *gain* strength and experience is to *not* run but to *fight* your way through it!

Don't let *defeat* or *failure* define *who* you are. Or you won't know how *successful* you could be!

If you want *change*, then you need to be the *one* to cause change. We say we want a *better* life. We want this. We want that. But some of us aren't doing *anything* but wishing and hoping. Successful people didn't wait for an opportunity to come. They went after an opportunity or just created one! Don't expect *success* to happen fast or for the journey to be smooth. *Pray* and take *risks*! If you do *little*, you get *little*! If you *want* more, then you *need* to do more!

Distractions are everywhere but stay *focused* on where you're heading to. Don't allow people or situations to run you off course. Follow God's leading. He won't lead you astray!

Whatever is happening in the world in general shouldn't be surprising. God already said in His Word that occurrences of all sorts would happen. I'm *not* going to stop enjoying my life because of what's going on around me. I'm still gonna work towards *reaching* my goals. As long as I'm living my life *acceptable* to God, I am *not* afraid to die!

Know that God is in *control* of whatever situation you may be in but *only* if you allow Him to be!

Don't be a person that waits for handouts! Go and *do* what you want to do and get to *where* you want to be! Timing depends on how *soon* you start making moves and how *consistent* you stay despite of setbacks and resources!

I'm on my way to *better* days! It doesn't matter what it *looks* like, seasons change!

Nothing is *impossible* when you include God in your plans. No matter how *much* you may have to *sacrifice*, no matter how *long* it takes, it is *possible*!

There is *no* situation that God can't help you with. Don't depend on yourself! God is all the assistance that you *need*! It will be taken care of once you *reach* out to Him!

Give your all to God for He has given His life for you!

If you stay *strong* and not *give up*, you'll know how it feels to be an *overcomer*!

Whatever choices or decisions I make now is going to benefit my future *not* just only for right now. Right now will be gone tomorrow!

Maybe certain things haven't happened for you because you didn't *ask* God for them. Or maybe you did pray and ask God for those things, but you still haven't received them yet. During the waiting period, you can easily become *impatient* and that could have a *huge* effect on your *faith* in God. Wait with *confidence* I say! God doesn't *break* His promises! It will come to pass!

It doesn't matter what you're going through, *you'll make it anyhow*!

It's so easy to talk about what we wish we *had* or what we wish we could *do*. But what *greater* feeling than to actually do something toward those dreams and goals? When you're doing something about it, it'll have you feeling more positive and start to excite you as you progress!

Your burning *passion* is your *calling*!

Some things we may want to do, we might have to wait a little while. But other things, we really just need to *go for it* and take a *leap of faith*! There may *never* be a *right* time all the time! Don't get me wrong. *Pray,* use *wisdom,* and *common sense,* but don't *waste* time either!

Be around people that are going to accept *every-thing* about you, *not* judge you for the way you are!

Love and *believe* in yourself and the things you can *accomplish*!

If you *need* God to come through for you, wait *patiently* and *confidently*!

God allows us to go through good times and bad times, but little do we know, He has to allow certain things to happen just to position us exactly where He wants us to be! Don't ever compare your journey with someone else's. God has different plans for each and every one of us!

Don't Worry. Worship!

DON'T WORSHIP YOUR PROBLEMS. Instead worship God, the One who can take your problems away. Stop giving your problems so much attention!

When you start *expecting* God to do *great* things in your life, then that's when *great* things will start happening for you. So question of the day, what are you *expecting* God to do for you? Are you expecting Him to do small, mediocre things or *great, mind-blowing* things?

Life is *not* easy, but when you have God in your life, He helps you get through the uneasy parts of life!

You need to know that there's *more* to life than what you see. God has so much *more* in store for you. What you see is *not* it! Your life has *purpose* whether you believe it or not. God can *use* you in ways you wouldn't even *imagine*. You need to *stop* being *negative* toward yourself and believe that *greatness* lives inside of you!

I am *who* God says I am, and I can *do* what God says I can *do*! We need to *ignore* what people say about us and *listen* to what God says about us!

When you don't expect *people* to reward you but instead expect *God* to reward you, you literally have *nothing* to worry about. We need to stop having *high* expectations for people. Expect your *blessings* to come from *above*!

If you really *want* something, you may have to *sacrifice* some things for it! Nothing comes for *free*, and nothing comes *easy*!

Keep reminding your *problems* how *big* your God is!

Why is it so hard to give God credit when good things happen to us? As if we got it all on our own. We would be *nothing* and have *nothing* if it wasn't for Him!

The best thing you can do is *be yourself*, and let the *right* people gravitate toward you! Everyone is *not* going to be in agreement with how you *think*, how you *speak*, or the *things* that you *do*!

Why is it so *easy* to talk about people but *difficult* to pray for them? We need to really *evaluate* ourselves. Stop praying *only* for yourselves. Everybody don't know God. Everybody *don't* know all the right things to *say* or to *do*. If we want to be *more* like God, we really need to look at the person or their situation and ask ourselves "WWJD?" What would Jesus do? We gotta do better people!

You need to have a *burning* desire to know God.

Instead of *asking* God for things, start *claiming* those things by *faith* and watch them become a *reality*!

It's up to you to do what's *right*! No one has *power* over you unless you give them that advantage. Your subconscious or your spirit will *always* tell you the *right* thing to do. That's why, at times, you *really* have to *ignore* your flesh. Your flesh most likely *won't* tell you the right things to think about or to do.

The *only* way to face a *problem* is to put a *praise* on it!

God knows my *heart*, and that I'm determined to be *who* He wants me to be. God is *not* saying I can't be myself. He just wants me to have His "characteristics" along with my personality. More of you, Lord, and *less* of me!

God is *not* expecting you to change your ways *overnight*. If He sees that you're actually *trying*, that's good enough for the time being. He can't help you unless He sees some type of *effort* that you're putting in. He's going to do His part most definitely, but *most* of the time, He's *waiting* on us to do our part first.

Change *won't* happen unless you really want it. You gotta get rid of *unhealthy* habits and addictions. *Clean up* your attitude and perspective toward life and people. Set goals and have a *game plan* on how to achieve them. You have to *do* something different in order to *get* different results! Doing the same thing, the same way *won't* always work for every situation. Step out in *faith* and do what *needs* to be done!

As long as you stay *productive*, you're *not* wasting time! It doesn't matter if you're working on something *big* or small. If it's going to help you move forward in life and *better* your future, it's a *life changer*!

Worrying kills your *faith*! Don't allow the main thing that can *help* you get through your situation and even *change* your situation get thrown out the window. Your *faith* is what makes things *happen*!

You can pray to God, but you still have to do your part. God is *not* going to do everything for you! You still have to put *effort* into the situation. You still have to *trust* and *have faith* in God. You still have to live right and be *obedient* to His Word in order to receive His blessings.

Blessings come in different forms. So be *open* and *grateful* whenever and however God blesses you!

When you decide that your relationship with God is *more* important than anything else, that's when you've really gotten your priorities in line.

Things happen for a reason, but you still gotta trust God!

Things will get *better* as long as you *believe* it will. What you *believe* matters!

Learn from your *mistakes* and make *better* decisions!

After you've prayed about something, you have to *believe* that God has already answered it.

When God says He's going to do something for you, you *better* believe it!

Find *joy* in every *bad* circumstance. Don't lose your *joy* because things aren't going good. Circumstances are *temporary* which means you shouldn't have to lose your *joy* and *happiness* for a moment that's *not* meant to last forever. Give your problems over to God and walk away smiling!

There is *nothing* you can't *overcome* with God's help. Ask for His help, and He will help you. Be *determined* to do what it takes.

You can *complain*, *complain,* and *complain*, but *nothing* is going to change unless you actually *do all that you can do*!

Things are getting *better* whether you see the changes or not. It's better to be positive while waiting, instead of being negative. It won't be easy, but it's good for you. Having *faith* is the only way you're going to get through your current circumstances.

First, listen then learn and then practice.

God is *not* ignoring your prayers. He'll answer them at the *right* time, so don't be discouraged.

Things don't just *suddenly* get better. It takes time. So be patient!

Your life is *not* falling apart. It's falling into place. Trust God!

Just because things get *rough* doesn't mean to give up and stop. Where do you think *strength* comes from?

Be grateful and thankful for what you have. There are people praying to have what you have. Don't look at it as little or simple. What you do have is a *blessing*!

You can't *pray* and then *worry*. You can't do *both*. Make up your mind! You either *pray* and have *faith* or *worry* and feel *hopeless*.

You may not know what's going on in your life, but at least God knows. He's working everything out for your good. Do what you have to do and leave the rest for Him to do.

Is there a *big* decision you may need to make soon, and you don't know exactly the right thing to do? This is the time to use wisdom and common sense. Pray, make a move, then Trust God.

It doesn't matter how God operates. He's still looking out for you and still blessing you. That's all you need to understand.

When you get into a new relationship with that special someone, acting all lovey-dovey, texting all day and night, can't wait until they call you, and you want to see each other every day, etc. People like to call that the "honeymoon" phase. That "honeymoon" phase doesn't have to only apply to new relationships/marriages. That "phase" doesn't have to "fade." Just because you two put in some years and think y'all know everything about each other doesn't mean you can't keep the fire burning. The "honeymoon" phase doesn't have to be just for the beginning. It's up to you to keep things the same if that's what you want for your relationship/marriage.

Your current circumstances *do not* determine your future. Your *faith* does!

A blessing is worth *keeping,* not worth *destroying*.

When you thought God didn't hear your prayers and then out of nowhere every single one got answered around the same time. We may not understand how God works, but when He does something for us, it's always *mind-blowing*!

Having *faith* will help you get through *great* difficulties and trials.

God is *always* near and at work in *your* life whether you believe it or not.

Fight to keep your happiness *no matter* what it takes. Life is too short to *not* enjoy this *one* life you *only* have.

To be spiritually fit, feed on God's Word, and exercise your faith.

Until God opens another door, tough it out! You can't keep running away all the time.

The time to live for Jesus is now.

Thank God for how He has provided in the past. Thank Him for what He will do. Ask Him what He wants you to do. Then trust Him.

Ladies, be with someone who already knows his identity. Someone who has confidence in himself. Someone that loves himself. If he takes care of himself very well, He'll take care of you even *better*!

Don't become nervous when God has brought something brand-new to the table. Take the challenge!

God is a *great* God! He will bless you in the midst of your circumstances just to remind you that He is still *God*, and that *He* is still in control. Just to remind you that He is still near. There is *no* problem or situation that's bigger than *God*! All things are working for your good!

The setbacks of life can teach us to wait upon the Lord for His help and strength.

Pray About Everything!

LADIES AND GENTLEMEN, THE wait is worth it! Don't let lonely nights discourage you. Have patience. If you don't have patience, pray for patience. Trust me, you don't want to invest into the wrong person. Don't let your temporary emotions take over and get you into some hot water. Don't jeopardize your heart again. You deserve God's best. If you're not desperate, waiting shouldn't be a problem. Focus on God and not on your circumstances. God knows what He's doing. Don't interfere with the blessings that He's trying to put together for you! Relax.

GOD SAYS TO "PRAY about everything. Fear nothing." He cannot work through your fears, but only if you would give Him your faith. He would help you in your situation. Isn't it good to know that God cares about everything that concerns you—even the little things you're afraid of? Your part is to pray and have faith, and God's part is to provide the power to meet your need. What do you need to pray about tonight?

When we put our problems in God's hands, He puts His peace in our hearts.

Encourage people. Empower people. Uplift people. Motivate people. Comfort people. Pray for people, and love people, but don't let their problems become *yours*! Let God handle the rest for them. You've done your part!

God has given us His Word to help us know and follow Him.

We as a people have the *wrong* mind-set about helping and serving others. We have become so selfish that we won't help others unless someone is helping us. When Jesus was on this earth, He came to serve. He never asked for anything in return. Yes, we have our own problems to deal with, but there is *always* something you can do to help someone else. God wants us to walk in His footsteps. He blesses those who are willing to be a blessing to others. I don't know about anybody else, but I'm going to continue to be a blessing to the people around me.

If the people you're hanging with are *not* supporting you, then they're just going to *try* to stop you. Be around people that are going to build you up *not* tear you down.

You gotta *believe* that things are already getting *better*!

Maybe if we mind our own business, other people's lives wouldn't affect us!

We need each other to get to where God wants us to go.

Staying positive will *always* get you through situations. Having the right *attitude* will keep you *focused* on the *right* things.

Things are probably coming together slowly, but at least they're coming together. Stop trying to rush things. Just be patient and wait!

Don't focus on what you *can't* do. Focus on what you *can* do, and let God handle the rest!

When you don't go looking for a blessing, blessings come and find you!

If you fully depend and trust people, you will be disappointed. But if you put your trust in God and fully depend on Him, He will *not* fail nor disappoint you. He will do just what He said He would do.

Make sure what you do is led by the Holy Spirit and *not* a fleshly desire.

Looking for someone who won't disappoint you? Look to Jesus.

Keep *pushing* until something happens! You won't know unless you *try*!

You gotta *believe* if you want *change*. If you don't *believe*, how can you expect *change*?

I'm *not* going to allow my current circumstances to discourage me. I serve a God that can change my situation at any time.

Why should I worry? That's when having *faith* should kick in.

Those that have the hardest struggles has the biggest purpose.

A man that *follows* God can *lead* me!

Jesus is looking for full-time followers!

Faith is seen in our actions.

You gotta *believe* that everything is going to be *all right* even if things aren't currently *right*!

Everybody is *not* going to want to hear the *truth*, but that doesn't mean the *truth* shouldn't be *told*!

Just to let you all know, this is how God works! What you do for Him, He'll do for you. If you're obedient to Him, He'll bless you. Nothing comes for free. So let me ask you this: Since God knows your needs and desires, are you doing your part so He can come through for you, or are you just expecting blessings without putting the work in?

Live with purpose! Seek God with all of your heart.

No matter what you're feeling right now, no matter how much others are discouraging you, don't give up on Jesus. Keep pressing forward, and don't give up hope!

Focus on succeeding at what God has called you to do, and stop being overly concerned about what other people think.

Choose kind and gentle words to uplift people and *kill* gossip!

Nothing I have, have I received on my own. God gets all of the *credit*!

I can honestly say when things look and seem *impossible.* God always shows up to remind me that I serve an *all-powerful* God, and that there is *nothing* that He cannot do! You might *not* be able to do a certain thing on your own, but God can get it done *for you*! Be blessed.

God wants you to do what's important in His eyes and laying aside your own personal feelings as to what's important. That's how you live a disciplined life for God. Jesus laid down His life for you, so He is asking you to lay down your interests for His greater cause.

Some of us got it *twisted*! God should be number one in your life! You need to *seek* God first before *any* man or woman. Until you do just that, don't *expect* anyone to come your way. Yes, God is a *jealous* God. And He wants to be your first love!

God will help you become all that He plans for you to be!

Don't allow *wealth* to get in the way of your relationship with God. Because you got *money*, you don't *need* God?

Just attending church is *not* enough! God is coming back for those who have a *real, intimate* relationship with Him. He's coming back for those who decided to *fully* dedicate their lives to Him.

Don't just read and study the Word. Be a doer of the Word. How can you grow if you don't put what you read into practice? God wants to use you, but you have to be obedient for that to happen. Speaking His Word over your life is what *makes* things *happen*!

Life is full of tests. If we don't pass one, we can't move on to the next one. Thank God, He lets us retake them until we get it right.

No matter how exhausted I may feel, God *always* gives me enough strength to do what I have to do. He knows how us humans eventually run out of gas, but He's always there to fill us back up to keep us going.

Don't give up because it seems like it's taking forever to get things done, long as you get them done!

God knows we're *not* perfect. But God forgives those who confess their guilt.

The devil wants to discourage you from believing that God is answering your prayers. Don't be discouraged when you're going through terrible trials. Always trust God to answer your prayers.

Get up every day and *do* your best, and then *trust* God for the rest.

Continue to do what you know is *right* to do regardless of how you *feel* or what you're going through.

Some of us are *expecting* God to throw us a *big* blessing every day. But we get a *daily* blessing which is waking up to see another day, but some people take that for granted as if they can control *life* and *death* themselves. If I don't get any other blessing today, I know that me being *alive* is the *biggest* blessing I've gotten today, and I'm fine with that.

We all want to do things our way, but God's way is *always* the best way.

Just because you don't know what's going on or don't understand, you gotta have *hope* and *faith*! You just have to believe that things will make sense in time.

When you *mind* your own business, how can you have *drama*? Maybe if you *invest* your time into yourself more, you'll have *no time* to worry about what's going on in *other* people's lives!

The devil can *start* his plans, but God won't let him *finish* it!

Do what you *can* do and allow God to handle what you *can't* do! There is *no* reason to be stressed!

I am *not* going to act like I can take care of myself and *fight* my own battles because I *can't*! *I need God!*

We look to see what other people are doing with their lives and wish we could do that too. But we all have our own destiny to fulfill. If you don't know what yours is, what a perfect time to pray and ask God about His plans for your life. You can try to follow your passions and dreams, but if that's *not* a part of God's will for your life, it won't happen. Proverbs 16:9 says, "We can make our plans, but the Lord determines our steps." Listen, *not* to sound harsh or discouraging but before we were ever created, His plans for our lives was *already* established. You just didn't know about them yet. But as of right now, just follow the path that He has set for you *right now*. In due time, you'll find out what your purpose is. Pray about it. His plans for your life will be satisfying.

Everybody has to walk down a *rough* road before it gets smooth. Hang in there!

Everywhere I go and everyone that I meet, I try to make sure people *see* God in me. I try to be a *light*. I try to make sure I rub off *positivity* on others. I just want to use my life to help others have a *better* life.

Put your *trust* in God. No one is going to look after you *better* than Him. I don't have time to be wondering and doubting. I need to know that somebody got me *covered* and that they're watching my back!

God loves you and cares about you. You can talk to anyone about your concerns, but *only* God has all the answers for you. God is *all ears*. Speak to Him. He's listening.

When you please people, you end up losing who *you are*. But when you please God, you end up becoming who you were *always* meant to be.

It doesn't matter how *big* or small my problems are. There's *nothing* my God cannot do!

I'm trying to do what most people won't do. Somebody has to "stand out" and do the impossible!

God will show you how to be strong in all areas of your life: mentally, emotionally, physically, and spiritually. But you won't find out unless you ask Him how. But just to give you a heads-up, everything is in the Word.

Rather than complain, pray! Then after you've prayed, wait!

When God sends the *right* people into your life, there's *no* drama coming with them.

If someone talks to you about *everybody*, then they are going to talk about you to *everybody*.

You gotta stay true to who you are and *not* allow people to make you who they want you to be!

I love that God puts pressure on us *not* to break us but for us to break out of our shells. God sees more in *you* than you see in *yourselves*. So He'll use certain tactics and situations to bring out those special abilities and gifts in you so that you can see what He sees.

Today, choose *not* to let people steal your joy. Choose to *focus* on getting what needs to be done. Ignore all foolishness. Today *will be* another *great* day!

As long as you stay positive, you have no choice but to succeed.

Another day to work toward your goals. Use your time wisely today. Every step you make, big or small, *counts*!

Not only do you need to have *faith* but you gotta speak the Word of God and *believe* what you're saying for things to happen. Once you start getting impatient and frustrated, you're interfering with your own blessings from getting through to you. Don't mess it up! Either you *believe* in God's Word or you're doubting it. You can't do both.

Don't think while you're *single* and *waiting* that there isn't anyone searching for someone like you. You are *valuable* and *special*. Not anybody deserves to be with you. You have so much *worth* that everybody won't see that! You are a buried *treasure*, and the *right* hunter will *discover* you!

Tonight, I pray that you *will* have a *better* week than last week. I pray that *this week* will be a *successful* week. I pray that *no matter* what happens, you *will* enjoy this week to the fullest. In Jesus name, I pray. Amen! If you *believe*, you shall *receive*!

Form Positive Habits!

Don't focus on your weaknesses. Focus on God!

Your words have amazing power so quit talking about what you can't do and start talking about what God can do. Keep your mind focused on God's goodness.

How much you own or how smart you are is not important. The most important thing is loving and obeying God.

God is in charge of all things. He sets a time for everything that happens. Things that don't seem fair will be made right in the future.

Never forget this: God knows your worth, and you know yours. So make sure whoever is really interested in you knows it too.

Rise and shine, beautiful women. This is a new day. Let nothing stop you from reaching your goals. You are strong and more than a conqueror. You will be all that you can be. You are limitless. Anything is possible if you put your mind to it. Tell yourself, "I will not give up!" You will continue to press forward through the stresses of life because you are blessed with God's inner strength. You can do it! You can make it! Now live out your life to the fullest today! And let nothing hold you back!

We don't deserve anything, yet God gives us everything!

I'm *not* perfect, but I rather form positive habits that will *only* help me succeed in my life. *Not* habits where it's destroying my life, causing problems in my body and affecting my mind, heart, and spirit, dragging me down deeper and deeper into a black hole. The things we do with our lives, we don't think about the consequences that can happen at that moment until we've done it for too long or just doing it at all for a short time, and then we realize that we have lost control of our own lives. Please, brothers and sisters, get rid of ungodly habits. If you know that there's a possibility that your actions can affect your life in a drastic way, don't wait until later to decide to stop. There might *not* be a later. Do what you need to do now so you can have a healthy, successful future.

I am going to enjoy life *without* doing things that are going to shorten my life span.

God *only* wants to do whatever He can do to help you become a *better* person. He wants to enhance *every* area of your life. He sees *great* potential in you that you might *not* see. You know that Satan will try to do just the *opposite*. Don't give into the *lies* of Satan. God will *use* you and *bless* you, *only* if you fully *dedicate* yourself to Him.

I refuse to quit just because I see obstacles ahead. I am *not* threatened by time. I will finish the race *no matter* how long I take. That trophy is mine before I even start!

Who God says I am, that's who I am. Your words have *no* power. I am *royalty* because my Father is the King of Kings and the Lord of Lords.

Don't be with someone that's going to separate you from God. Be with someone that's going to make you want to get even closer to Him.

When you pray to God about your concerns, you gotta believe that *change* is coming. Tonight, choose to relax and to sleep in peace. Stressing will *not* change anything but will make your problems seem *bigger* than what it really is. I'm praying for you all.

It's awesome to know that if we trust God with our lives, He'll take care of us and safely lead us to prosperity and success!

Have a *determined* heart and *be* the *best* that you can be.

Dating advice: place God first in every aspect of your life including your dating life. He deserves first place, and any relationship that doesn't put Him there is the wrong relationship for you.

God hears your prayers, but do you have *enough* patience to wait for them to come to pass?

You have to wake up and tell yourself how you *expect* your day to be. Yes, unexpected situations pop up, but are you going to let those surprise situations steal your joy and peace? Your attitude determines the outcome of your day! Try to make today the *best*!

Ladies and Gents, you can't just be with someone just because you're attracted to each other and got a little chemistry going on. The real question is, what else can you both offer other than that? Are you or them bringing growth to each other in positive ways? Do they see life the way you see it? Do you have anything in common? There is obviously more important questions other than these that I've listed, but these questions really do matter and will determine who you invest your time into. You can't waste time unless you ask questions. Don't put yourself into a situation where you're saying to yourself later on "I didn't know they were like that or felt that way." The more you know, the better the decisions you will make.

Be around people that are going to keep you on the *right* path, *not* steer you off into a ditch!

God *never* told us to fight our own battles. We're *not* equipped for all of that. All He wants us to do is speak His Word and *trust* in Him. He will do the fighting. You're getting stressed out for no reason. Keep your *peace* and stop trying to be your own hero!

Your *blessings* are closer than you think. This dry season that you're in, you're coming out!

It's a *new day*, and God has already provided *enough* strength for you to get through the day. But you have to believe that you *will* make it!

Believe you are *blessed* before those *blessings* come! Show your *confidence* in God early!

Believe it or *not*, the Word of God and your *faith* are the strongest weapons you've got. Don't give them up!

God is going to have us at places where we don't want to be, doing things we don't want to do. But it's only leading us to where He wants us to actually be. Don't expect a straight and easy path there. We're going to be all over the place before we get to our final destination. But remember, He will be with you every step of the way. You will *not* be alone! Trust in His way of doing things.

If Christ is the center of your life, you'll always be focused on Him.

If you know God, you'll never walk alone!

God loves you despite of your sins. God loves you despite of all your past mistakes. Never feel that God doesn't love you because you're *not* perfect! He's *not* asking for you to be perfect. Come to Him just the way you are. Don't feel as if He can't use you to do great and amazing things because you feel that you've done too much wrong. It doesn't matter how far you try to run away from Him or how many times you fail Him, He still loves and cares about you!

The *right* one will continue to express their love to you from the first day to the end! Real feelings won't fade because you're in a relationship or a marriage. How you got them is how you'll keep them if it was *real* to begin with.

There is *nothing* wrong with being attracted to someone. But the *bond* has to be there in order for the relationship to last. Too many people are getting into relationships for the *wrong* reasons but get mad when things don't work out. Check your motives!

We sit here and allow ourselves to drown in our circumstances while God is simply asking us, "Where is your faith? Haven't I come through for you many times before?"

People tend to *forget* that God is with us during our storms. He allows things to happen for a reason. But we still ask God, "If you really love me, then why are you letting me go through all of this?" Stop *questioning* Him and start *trusting* Him.

Speak God's Word over your life, *believe* it and *not* doubt it. And then watch Him work!

Nothing better than having a friendship and a relationship with the One you truly love. Having the best of both worlds makes it even better!

Guard your *mind*! Nobody is perfect, but don't allow your *thoughts* to get out of control. Unhealthy thoughts are *dangerous*! Monitor your attitude. Your attitude can either bring *positivity* to your life or *negativity*. If your thoughts and attitude are offtrack, you will end up doing something *you will* regret. Control your *actions*. Don't allow people, things, or situations to cause you to act out of character. The guilt and shame *always* kicks in after it's all said and done. Don't lose your *peace*. Be cautious, and if you feel yourself drifting, *tap* out and get back on track immediately.

We will have to go through *situations* that we don't want to go through and do things we prefer *not* to do, but *trusting* God is all that we *can* do. Expect that God will *reveal* to you why you had to have those *experiences* because it will all make sense in the end.

Your attitude determines how far your *faith* will go. Do you *trust* that God will live up to His promises? Are you *expecting* God to come through for you? No matter how long He takes, don't let your *faith* run out!

If my life is affected by the choices I make, I rather make the *right* choices because guess what? I gotta deal with whatever consequences that comes with it, *not* anybody else.

I rather please God than people. My life is in His hands and *not* in anybody else's.

During those *tough* times is when you *need* your *faith* the most! Don't *lose* something that's going to help you get *through* it.

Sometimes we forget what God has already blessed us with. Why don't we just be grateful and thankful for our "right now" blessings while we're waiting for our other blessings to come through. Yeah, let's try doing that!

When you're doing the *right* thing, you can't help but smile from within.

Relationship advice: Make Bible study a team sport. When two people study the Word together, God blesses them and their relationship.

What's awesome is when God confirms something to you. There's nothing you or anybody could say to change what's been spoken and revealed to you. It is what it is. It's written in stone!

Everybody needs God in bad times, but when things are all good, He's not even on your mind at all. Yet He still listens to your prayers and wants to give you the best of life. God's love is so beyond human love. God is not going to choose who He's going to love and who He's not going to love. He just loves all no matter how you treat Him.

The *right* people *only* want to bring out the good in you. They only want to see you *succeed* in life. They are *not* after what's yours. They will see something *special* in you and *only* want to bring it out! People, you gotta *realize* who's with you for the good and who's not! It's actually *not* complicated to figure it out. They either help you *become* a better person and support your dreams, or they're bringing *drama* into your life and throwing your past in your face!

Have faith in what you're believing God to do for you. Without faith, how can you expect change? You gotta put your all into what you believe in. All or nothing!

This is a brand-new week so *expect* brand-new things to happen!

Thank God for "closed doors" because you might not have wanted to deal with what was behind them!

When you're patient and willing to wait, everything will happen exactly how it's supposed to!

Don't give up—God hears you when you pray!

Ladies, if a guy is serious about you, he will *not* play games with you. You will be *pursued*! You will become a *priority* in his life. There will be *no* secrets! He will be *open* and *honest* about everything with you. He will let you know that you are *included* in his future plans. *Point-blank, period!*

God is the *only* one who can change your circumstances around. He is the *only* one who knows all. He has the *solution* to every problem. You don't have all the answers, but He does! Let Him do His job! He's waiting for you to turn everything over to Him so He can get to work!

Do not worry about tomorrow. Give your problems over to God for He cares for you. Tonight, relax and get some rest while God is preparing tomorrow for you!

Someone who sees *value* in you is *worth* being with!

We are blessed if our confidence is in the Lord!

Lord, I want *more* of you than *anything* else! My life filled with you. I'll have *everything* that I could ever *need* and *want*!

When you're focused on God and enjoying your life, that's when God gives you the desires of your heart. You know why? Because you're spending time with Him, being content with what you have and still enjoying life even though you don't have everything that you want at the moment. But God loves to bless people when they least expect it. What better feeling than having surprise blessings.

God's *test* will be my *testimony*!

What I *go* through, I will *grow* through!

If you don't wait, you'll get what you *don't* deserve. If you do *wait*, you'll get exactly what you deserve!

Ladies, a man cannot lead us if he is *not* being led by God! Never forget that.

I have a dream, and I am determined to see it fulfilled.

Stay on your A game! If you hear negative thoughts in your head or if someone is speaking negative things to you, you know that's the enemy trying to discourage you. He's trying to break you down, and you cannot allow let him get away with that. If you want God's best, speak life over yourself. Speak positive words into your mind. "And we know that God causes everything to work together for the good of those who love God and are called according to his purpose for them" (Romans 8:28). No one, *not* even the "enemy," can get in the way of God's plan for you. *Not* your friends, *not* your family, *not* your coworkers, *not* your ex-girl-friends/ex-boyfriends, and definitely *not* your haters. I am here to tell you that your future is *set*!

God wants us to pray before we do anything at all.

Listen people, being a Christian and living by the Bible is *not* a whole bunch of *rules* and *regulations*. When you come to know Christ, what's right is *right*, and what's wrong is *wrong*. Your mind-set will eventually *start* to change as you continue to *study* the Word of God. Things that you *used* to do that weren't good will become things that you *no longer* crave or have interest in. All things become *new*! But only if you *really* want to form a *real, intimate* relationship with Christ will you *understand* how the transformation works! But that's up to you, *no pressure*!

Never *lose* sleep when God is *already* working everything out for *your* good! Get some rest!

Don't invest time into someone that is *not* investing time into you!

God *never* said we had to *fight* our own battles! When we *give* our problems to Him, it's already *done*!

Single ladies, there's *nothing* wrong with *desiring* to date or to get married. I just want you to *avoid* saying "you're lonely" just because you *don't* have a man in your life. Stop saying you're lonely because you don't have a guy to talk to on Friday and Saturday nights on the phone. Happiness does not come from being with a man. You can be unhappy in a relationship as well. You are *not* lonely or alone! You have *God*. You have *family*, and you have *friends*. You *need* to be *content* with where you are in your life right now. *Enjoy* life by yourself *first* before God *blesses* you to enjoy and to share it with someone else!

Where God places you, He will take care of you!

Sometimes in the *end*, all you end up having is your *faith*! Don't *lose* it!

Your *past* does *not* define *who* you are *today*! You are a *flower* that has grown through *concrete*! Don't *allow* anyone to *hold* you down by your *past* because you've decided to become a *better* person and to make *better* decisions.

Make a *move* and *see* what happens! You can't get a *reaction* without taking *action*!

Never underestimate God and the way *He* does things. Whatever He does, *always* turn into something *incredible*! So despite of what you *may* be going through right now, He is right there with you!

It's *always* good to know someone *superior* has control over your life other than you because *we* don't have *all* the answers. But God does!

Ladies, there is *no* need for competition or *trying* to be like the next woman. Just know what God has for you is for you *only*! Don't *waste* your time worrying about another *woman* that ain't paying your bills. You go and get yours! You do what's *best* for you and your situation!

Happiness *always* starts with you *first*! Don't depend on *people* or *materialistic* things to bring *happiness* into your life!

Make it a habit to pray before you lay! If God continues to give you *breath* every morning, let Him know you are *grateful* and *thankful* by saying a *simple* prayer before you rest at night!

Sometimes you just gotta *look* at things in a *different* perspective! Seeing things in a new *way* can bring new *understanding*!

Start *expecting* good things to *happen* for you! What's to lose? Let this week be *better* than last week. God is going to *bless* you! Are you *ready*?

People are *only* jealous of you because you have *something* that they want. But *when* did that ever *become* your problem?

If you're going through some difficulties right now, I want to tell you this: There is *no* alcohol that can wash down your problems. There is *no* cigarette or herb that could smoke your problems away and poof they're gone. There is *no* drug that you can *take* or *inject* that could *cure* what's wrong. Ladies, there is *no* man that makes *anything* better. Guys, there is *no* woman that can *change* your situation. At the end of it, *all* you have is *Jesus*! Go to Him instead of these temporary fixer-uppers aka solutions. Take your problems to the *One* who can *take* them away! He's here, and He's ready to listen to you whenever you're ready. *No rush!*

FORM POSITIVE HABITS!

Just because you *can't* do it now doesn't mean you'll *never* be able to do it!

I believe people that *don't* have anything *going* for their lives will *always* be *concerned* about yours.

Why *continue* to do something that you know you *shouldn't* be doing just to *feel* bad about it afterwards? When is it going to *click* in your head to stop?

Don't *ask* God for things, and once He *blesses* you with them, He gets *kicked* to the curb. God *wants* to give you the *desires* of your heart, but He is *not* dumb. If you *don't* receive them, maybe it's because He *knows* you'll make those things *more* important than Him. You *need* to make a decision *who's* going to be number one in *your* life!

Waiting on *your* blessings *only* tests your *patience* and *faith* for God! Will you *last* through the *waiting* period?

You *won't* make it in this world *without* God! Put your *faith* and *trust* in Him! Trusting God through your *tough* times will only *make* you spiritually *stronger*!

Be with someone that wants to *pull* you into their life because they *want* you there. They will *make* room to *fit* you right in. You will have a *reserved* spot in their life. You shouldn't have to *force* or try to *fit* yourself into their life. If you have to do that, then you're *obviously* not that important to them. You deserve *better* than that. And another thing, *don't* wait for them to try to *make* time for you either. You will *never* know when that will happen. It's so *important* to get to know someone as *friends* before you even *think* about the next level. Being friends is like a *preview* to what to expect in a relationship. If they *can't* set aside time for you now, what makes you think things will be *any* better in a relationship?

Exercising your *faith* builds *spiritual* muscles!

Never let your *struggles* strip away your *strength*. Let your *struggles* create more *strength* to help you get *through* whatever that you're facing! *You will make it*!

Be *prepared* so when God puts you in the *right* place at the *right* time, provision and opportunities can *come* to you.

Surround yourself with people that *won't* cause you to do things that go *against* your *morals* and *standards*! Be around *like-minded* people!

You *can't* make *any* progress if you don't get *rid* of *bad habits* that are *preventing* you from moving forward.

God doesn't allow *temptations* into *your* life just to make you weak. He *allows* them *only* to see how much you *love* Him! Will you *fight* your *fleshly* desires for God?

I *may* have problems but I'm gonna *praise* my way *through* them *instead* of letting them bring me *down*!

God is a *God* of *justice*!

Trust me, you *will* get back *everything* you have lost! You *will* get what you *deserve*! It's *not* over *yet*!

We must grow through the pressures of life to help develop our character and strength. We will rise through the toughest and roughest situations just to bloom into the person we were always meant to be.

God will *always* love you *more* than *anyone* else!

His love is *endless*! He loves you *despite* of what you've *done* in your past or what you're doing now! He will *never* stop loving *you*! Don't forget that!

Whatever God allows us to go through is *never* intended to harm us. There is a *reason* for all situations and circumstances.

Sometimes you gotta *preach* to yourself and *remind* yourself what God's *promises* are for you! God *never* lies about what He says He'll do for you!

Do you want to get to *know* God so that you can *hear* from Him? Start by spending *time* with Him:

1. Pray.
2. Read the Bible.

You *can't* get to know someone if you *don't* spend *quality* time with them. It all *depends* on how serious you are about *developing* a relationship with Him.

Being a child of God, you have the *best* insurance coverage! God protects you from *anything* to *everything*! He's got you *fully*, 100 percent covered!

If people can't *handle* who you are, then they *gotta* go! Everybody *can't* be in your life. Everyone is on *different* maturity levels. Some *may* clash with others, and that's normal, but they gotta go if they can't *keep* up!

Surround *yourself* with people that *will* have a *positive* influence on you and your life. If they *can't* help you *shine* bright, then you're *plugged* into the *wrong* source.

Real love and care is when you're *not* trying to make a person *change* for you but because you *care* about their *soul,* their *life,* and the *decisions* that they make! It's *not* about you but about *them*! That's when it's *real*! Be with someone that will *help* you become a *better* person!

Don't wait for people to tell you that you have *greatness* inside of you! See that for *yourself*! Everyone is *not* going to notice all the *great* things about you. *Look* in the *mirror,* and you'll see for *yourself* that you are *gifted, talented,* and have *great* purpose for *your* life!

Fear keeps you in some real *bondage*!

Fear keeps you in a *box*!

Fear *discourages* you!

Fear *limits* you!

Fear is a *lie*!

Fear is a *dream crusher*!

Fear *affects* how you *see* yourself!

Fear affects your *self-esteem* and *self-confidence*! Fear can *change* who you really are. Don't allow *fear* to have *full* control over *your* life. You will go *nowhere* if *fear* exists inside of you!

Don't *beat* yourself up if you feel like you *didn't* accomplish a lot today. As long as you did something, *that's something*! Some people *don't* do anything and still *expect* results. It *doesn't* work that way. Give *yourself* some credit! Don't be *too* hard on yourself. Even if you're *limited* and *can't* do much right now, baby steps *will* eventually *add up*!

No matter *how* many enemies you *may* have, God has you *covered*! They *won't* lay a finger on you. They can't *touch* you! You're *not* just an ordinary person, you're a child of God! You are automatically *protected*. But don't get me wrong, people *will* try you, but they *won't* get away with it!

I love that God *fights* my battles so I don't have to *break* a sweat!

But God is *turning* things around for *you*! It doesn't matter *how* things look now because it *won't* be that way for long. God is *guiding* you *through* your problems and struggles. He's *holding* your hand *through* it all. You are *not* alone in this journey. He is *taking* you where He *wants* you to be, and you *will* get there!

Because you *can't* see the blessing yet, doesn't mean it's *not* coming! Have *faith*!

No *matter* what you're going through, it *doesn't* come to *stay*. It comes to *pass*!

Don't get *lost* in the crowd *trying* to be like everybody and *do* what everybody else is doing. Be your own *product*!

If you *want* something so bad, you gotta *tell* yourself you won't *stop* until you get it!

Don't think that your life is so *messed* up that God can't *fix* it. God can make it *beautiful*!

Don't go *back* to what you *prayed* to God to *help* get you out of!

No *matter* how long it *may* take for us to receive our blessings, God doesn't *break* His *promises*!

Whatever goals and dreams you *may* have, make sure you go to the *right* source for help which is *God*! He has *all* of all the necessary *connections* and *resources* that you *may* need to kick-start *whatever* you are trying to accomplish. When God is in it, *anything is possible*!

If someone is *really* interested in you, they wouldn't *question* your lifestyle and beliefs. They wouldn't question your morals, values, and standards trying to change *who* you are. If the interest is *real*, they would *accept* everything about you. If you and that person *don't* see things eye to eye, then it's *not* meant. Don't *try* to force things to work. If it *was* meant, things would be *lined* up the way it should be.

God *hears* our prayers. Once your *prayer* has been answered, don't play around with it and *not* take what's been *given* to you seriously. Now that's how you *ruin* blessings and opportunities!

Don't think that God is just *allowing* you to go through all kinds of *hell* just because He's using *you* for a reason. The devil knows that you're *strong*. He just doesn't want you to *figure* that out for yourself. If God says you're *strong*, then that's what *you are*!

We all say we *need* to *get away* because of the *stress* and *frustrations* of the world when all we *need* to do is *spend* time with God.

God should be your *getaway*. You can go *anywhere* in the world and *still* come back to the same *mess* you left. All you *need* to do is find a quiet place and just talk to God. Reading the Word *will* answer some questions that you *may* need. You gotta start somewhere. So start with God!

God works in *mysterious* ways!

In order for God to get us to the place that He wants us to be, He is *not* going to do things *normal* and *ordinary* sometimes. It's *not* always going to be a *straight shot* to that place. God *may* have us doing *zigzags* just to get us there.

But the *best* part about the *journey* is that God is *with* us *through* all the twists and turns and dead ends. Let God continue to *navigate* your life!

If you're *stuck* in a situation and don't know *how* it's going to turn out, it's *best* to just tell yourself, "The Lord is gonna work it all out!" Just keep it *simple*!

Whatever you're going through right now, *don't give up!* Once you give up, the *devil* has *won!* If you don't give up, you are *claiming* your *victory* in advance! Don't *throw* in the towel because your situation seems too *big* or too *hard* to overcome. There is a *great* abundance of *strength* inside of you. All you *need* to do is *believe* and *activate* it. You'll be surprised how *strong* you really are.

We often make *poor* decisions because we're *lacking* wisdom. We get so *caught up* in our circumstances trying to *figure* things out, *fix* things, and *make* things happen on our *watch* that we don't even *stop* and *pause* for a second just to *pray* and *talk* to God about it first. We make decisions *quick* without giving thought about it. It is *very important* to be led by the *Holy Spirit* in all that we do. *Yes!* In all that we do! Sounds extreme huh? But guess what? God knows *best*! We're *humans,* and we're going to make *mistakes,* but do you want to have *poor judgment* in everything? Trust God to lead you to make the *right* decisions!

Stop trying to *figure* things out! If you catch your-self trying to put the *pieces* to your *puzzle* together, you're going to be the *one* that causes *extra* stress upon yourself. All God asks you to do is to have *patience*, *faith*, and *trust* in Him. Is that *too much* to ask for?

We all at some point have to go *through* and *face* certain situations. We *might* not know why God *allows* it to *happen,* but there's a *reason* and a *purpose* behind it all. Trust God in all things and lean *not* into your own understanding!

Ever thought of *helping* someone else out while God is *working* out your current situations? What else better is *worth* doing while you're waiting? Is it *really* all about you? Don't you think God's *intentions* were for us to *care* for one another since we are *brothers* and *sisters* in Christ? Give whatever you can give whether it's *money*, your *time*, encouraging words, or just a *listening* ear. Invest in someone's life today!

When *all* things fail, God *never* fails! God is really a *true* father and a *true* friend! If anyone, I put *all* of my *trust* in His hands.

The *things* that we *go* through, if it *wasn't* for God, we would be *somewhere* having a *meltdown*!

In due time, the *right* doors will open up for you. God is a *very* organized person, and He is going to do *whatever* He needs to do for things to *happen* His *way*! If you don't have patience, you're in deep water! You *need* to pray and ask God to provide patience to you in *every* area of your life. Trust me, you're gonna *need* a whole lot of it!

Contentment comes when you *appreciate* what you *do* have, but you're *believing* God for *better*!

If you really want God's *best* and you *trust* that He knows who's *right* for you, you wouldn't be *impatient*! Still *enjoy* your singleness and continue to *prepare* yourself for your *future* mate. Every little preparation *counts*! You *don't* have to have someone just to enjoy life. Learn to *enjoy* yourself before enjoying someone else's company.

Find your *identity*! Don't allow other people to find it for you! Your identity is like your driver's license. Once you have it, it's yours to keep. Be who you are. Don't change for anyone because guess what? Everyone will *always* have their own opinion of who they think you should be. You can only be *you*! Don't let your license (identity) be suspended (reputation messed up) because you listened to people around you and didn't have the guts to just stay true to yourself. Fight the pressures of the world! You're *strong* enough!

What God has for you, it is *for you*! God wants to give you the *best*! So continue to be patient. You'll be glad that you *waited*!

No one deserves *success* without *hard work*! You *need* to know how it feels to *struggle*, to have *disappointments* and *failures*! You *need* to know how it feels to *start* from the *bottom* with *nothing* to deserve *something*! There's a *lesson* in everything!

Don't go to bed tonight *stressed* out. Give your concerns over to God and let Him work *everything* out. It's *not* for you to try to *fix* everything by yourself. Give it to the *expert*!

If you have people in your lives that are *not* helping you succeed in life, you need to *cut* them *off*! Are they *worth not* reaching your goals because of their *negativity* and lack of *support*? You have *dreams* to catch! Keep it *moving*!

Whatever you are *facing* right now, you have the *strength* to overcome whatever it is. There is so much strength *inside* of you that you *don't* even know about. *Activate it now!* Don't allow your current *circumstances* to bring you *down* to your knees or *push* you into a corner! You're *stronger* than this! So *act* like it!

Isn't God *good*? God is *always* on time!

Never *doubt* God's timing!

When you *put* God first in *your* life, then you're living *your* life *right*! Things *will* properly fall into place! Get your *priorities* in line!

People think Christians got it *all* together, but we *don't*! We're *struggling* just like *everybody* else. We *speak* the Word over our lives. We speak *faith*! We just put our *trust* in God and *not* in money or people. *Big difference!*

You *may* have *a lot* of things that you're trying to get *done*, and *money* is the primary *factor*. You might *not* be able to get *everything* done all at once like you *want* to, but it's *better* to get them done *no matter* how long it takes. Even if it's one by one or two by two.

Don't *lose* sight on the *many* blessings that are *surrounding* you! You *may* not see them, but they are there!

If someone is *interested* in you, they wouldn't want *anybody* else but *you*! It would be *something* special about you that they just can't *shake* off! It *will* keep them gravitating to you *no matter* what!

Please, people, while you're *driving* in your lane towards your *destiny*, do not *allow* distractions to have you *pull over* from staying *focused* on where you're *heading*. Don't become *curious*! Everything and everyone is *not* for you! Trust me, the *desires* of your heart *will* meet you at *your* destination. Stay *focused*!

You have to *believe* before *seeing* anything. Faith will *acknowledge* the truth of the Word of God where there is *no* sign to prove it. *Faith* doesn't *flow* in the *same* channel as the *human* senses. The point of *believing* is the point of *receiving*. *Unleash* your *faith* for *definite* results!

Don't be doubtful, *believe*! Everything begins with *faith*. You must *build* your faith *strong*! Remember, without *faith,* it is impossible to please God.

Faith speaks in *confidence*! It is born out of a *heart* which is full of *conviction* of the truth of the Word of God. *Faith* is not *swayed* by the *surroundings* and *noisy* circumstances.

Faith is a defense *against* circumstances that are meant to *discourage* you. It is a *shield* that beats the *fiery* darts of the enemy *hands* down. You will *advance* in this season; you will see the *hand* of God over you as you start *walking* and *speaking* in *faith*. Your life will be a *testimony*; the *celebrations* are in your *house* this time around. You *will* tell others of the *goodness* of God.

Walk by *faith* and *not* by *sight*! The eyes of *faith* will always *collect* what they see. Don't ever allow your *natural* sight to be *stronger* than your *faith*. Whatever the situation, your *faith* can *triumph* over it.

No *matter* what you've *done* in the *past*, God *will* not hold it against you. People *will!* Religion makes you *feel* guilty about *everything*, but just having a *relation-ship* with God puts the *focus* on continuing to *grow* with Him. He knows it's *not* an easy *journey*, but He's *willing* to stand by you every *step* of the way. God is a *forgiving* God and wants you to *come* to Him just the way you *are!* You can't *clean* up *your* life without Him. You *need* Him to *transform* your life. Don't *wait!* Let Him become *a part* of your life *today!* No *rush*, just take little steps day by day with Him and *watch* your life *change* in so *many* ways! Will you take that *step* of *faith* today? What's to *lose?*

You don't have to *wait* until you get that *car*, that new *place*, that new *career*, your college *degree*, that new *woman* or *man* in your life to appreciate what you have. Everything you have should be *appreciated*. No matter how *big* or *small* it is. Be *thankful* and be *grateful!* There is *someone* out there that doesn't have the things you have! You could easily *fall* into a *lower* position in *your* life if you don't take care of what you have.

There's nothing *wrong* with getting to know someone. If they're not the *right* one, that person should just remind you of who you *do* want.

If God gives you an *assignment*, then that means you're *capable* of doing it. Mute your *flesh* and *tune* into *your* spirit. He *wouldn't* open up a *door* for you if He didn't think that you were ready for it. If God says you're *ready*, then you *need* to be on the same page as Him and know that you're ready too! If God has *confidence* in you, then you *need* to have confidence in *yourself*! Time to *take charge*!

Being *open* and *honest* with yourself is the *first* step to *change*. You have to get *rid* of denial. As long as you stay in denial, you will *never* be *free*! You will *never* grow. You have to accept your *flaws* and be *willing* to make some changes. Making changes is a *good* thing. It is a *positive* choice to make. We have to *grow* every day. We can't just stay the same. We must get *better* and be *better*!

God is *not* going to bless you until you *make* Him number one in *your* life and *give* Him your *attention*! He knows your *needs* and the *desires* of your *heart*, but He *needs* for you to *focus* on Him and ignore the *distractions* around you. It's going to *feel* like nothing is *happening* for you until you *make* something *happen* which is getting your *priorities* in line. Will you *make* that *change*?

God allows us to go through *a lot* of different situations as a way for us to *grow* but also to *share* our *testimony* with others. *Look* around you! It may be *someone* that's about to put themselves in a *situation* that you've *already* been through. Or they are *experiencing* a situation which you have experienced already in the *past*. Share *your* testimony! Encourage them! Let them know what God has *done* for *you* when you were in that situation. Just be *real*! Don't allow a *brother* or a *sister* in Christ to go through *unnecessary* situations if you can help them *avoid* it! Save a *soul*!

Actions speak *louder* than words. There's *a lot* of talking but *no* walking. If you *mean* it, you'll *show* it!

Practice being *happy* for people for once! *Cut* down on the *jealousy and envious* attitude! Everything we go through and *experience* is a *test*! If God puts you in situations where you see people around you getting blessed, *you're next*! Be *happy* for them so others can be *happy* for you when your *time* comes around!

Be the *best* that you can be and *do* the *best* that you can do! Effort is what *counts*! Effort is what brings *change* and *results*! Don't *complain* if you're *not* doing anything! Make a *move*!

Are you believing for a *miracle* today? God can do *wonders*! He can change your situation within *seconds*!

Enjoy where you are in *your* life right now because it *will* get *better*! Make the *best* of *your* current situation. Make it *easy* on *yourself* while you're *waiting* to be upgraded to another *level* in *your* life!

People are entering *your* life every day! They are there for a *reason*. But once you find out what their *purpose* is later on, how *exciting* is that? Especially when they are there to help *push* you *forward*, not to *tear* you down or to *mess* anything up for you! God orchestrates situations so *perfectly*!

Things *won't* make sense in the beginning and while you're going *through* the process. And I can tell you this: You *won't* like the process either! But it *will* make sense once you get through it all in the end! What an *amazing* moment that would be to *look* back on and think. God knew what He was doing in my life. That's why this happened, that's why that happened! That's why I had to go through all that *mess* and had to deal with those people. It *all* makes *sense* now! You gotta *trust, trust, trust* in God!

When you're going through a lot, reading the Bible gives you this peace of mind that *nothing* else can give. Your problems may still be there, but reading the Bible helps guide you through *your* obstacles. Who else or what else could give *better* wisdom than the Word of God?

Lord, thank you for what you've *done* for me in the *past*, what you're going to do for me in my life *now* and in my *future*!

Lord, I may be struggling just like everyone else, but I *will* continue to keep the *faith* and know that *change* is coming! When your *blessings* start rolling into my life, I *will* be as *humble* as possible because I know the situations I had to *endure* just to get to that *high* place in my life. I *won't* allow having an *ego* or being *conceited* to get in the way of me being grateful and appreciative.

I pray that this week *will* be the best week that you've *ever* had! Favor *will* rest upon you. Needs *will* be met! Relationships that were broken, *mended*! Sick bodies, *healed*! Breakthroughs and "suddenlies" now *will* happen in *your* lives.

As *crazy* as this may sound to some, enjoy *your-self* while God is getting *your* future together. I mean, through the *good* and *bad*, still *enjoy* life! Continue to have that *hopeful* and *optimistic* attitude. Don't *waste* time worrying about things. God has it *all* under *control!*

Seasons *change*. Friends *come* and *go*. Don't feel bad or down because you're *not* close to certain people anymore. God places people in *our* lives for a *reason* and for a *season*. There was *purpose* in why you were in their *lives*. But if things have *changed* and the vibe is *not* the same anymore, that could possibly mean your *time is up* with them. It's time to *move on* to other people. Await *your* next assignment with God!

WHO WERE YOU YESTERDAY?

Be careful of *who* you call *your* friend! Just because that person is nice and friendly doesn't mean you can *label* them as a *friend*. Some people are trying to enter *your* life because of maybe your *looks* or what you *have*. Some people are there to *use* you so they can get to the *top* then *leave* you. It's *rare* to find *real, true* friends that just want to be in *your* life just to see you become *successful*! It's *rare* to find friends that just want to be a *support* system for you. That they just want to see you *blessed* and *happy* and don't want *anything* in return.

The *only* way to create more people like that is to *become* one *yourself*!

Don't *give up* because it seems like you're *losing*. It's just the beginning! You *will* win in the end!

Never *stop* praying even if your prayers haven't been *answered* yet. Show *consistency*! When you have *faith* in something that you're asking God for, you *shouldn't* stop! Don't get *discouraged* because it hasn't happened yet!

God *always* makes a *way*! God is *enough* for me! What else *more* could I ask for? Why depend on others who are *limited* by their abilities when you have a *limitless* God who can do the *impossible*?

If you are *single*, I encourage you to use this time wisely. Work on problem areas that you may have. Look back into *your* past relationships and whatever went wrong on *your* end, don't *repeat* it. We all like to complain and say, "We didn't do anything wrong, and that it was all the other person's *fault*!" That's probably *true*, but there are *still* some things you could have done *differently* as well. When God blesses you with the *one*, you need to be *better* than how you were back then. Make *better* decisions. Have a *better* attitude. Just be a *better* you!

Get *your* life together so God can start bringing new opportunities into *your* life! Do whatever you *need* to do to get on track. Don't forget that you don't have to do it alone! God is here to help you!

There's *nothing* wrong with asking people for *advice*. But at the end of the day, the decision is *still* left up to you. Follow *your* heart! Trust *your* own instincts! Do what *you* feel is *right*! Pray for *wisdom*!

Things *will* get better! It's better to be able to pay *your* bills and be broke after than to be broke and *not* be able to pay *any* bills! Be thankful for *that*! This is *only* a season that you're in. This is *not* the end! God is preparing *your* financial breakthrough *right now*! Yes, we are living in *hard* times, but God *will* provide, and He will *always* make a way out of *no* way!

235

You can't get anywhere *unless* you stay *consistent*! I know it's hard. The enemy knows your plans. He knows that you're trying to have a *better* life. He is trying to do *all* that He can to slow you down or if possible put a halt on you! Practice resilience, perseverance, and work on your endurance. If life knocks you down, *get back up and try again*! If you're trying to get back into school, *keep trying*! If you're trying to get a job, *keep trying*! If you're trying to get a car, *keep trying*! If you're trying to work on your relationships between family and friends, *keep trying*! If you're trying to start your own business, *keep trying*! I can't express these words more than this, *keep trying*! Taking action and being consistent, you *will* see results if you're still in motion. No more breaks, no more laziness, no more procrastinating, no more depending on someone to pump you up. *Just move!*

You need to be able to encourage yourself because it's not going to always be someone around to do that for you all the time. As long as you keep stalling, your blessings *will* just be sitting on the shelf dusting.

There are areas within us that we *need* improvement in. That's when God will put or allow you to be in *certain* situations to improve and to gain experience. There are *always* things about us that we need some work done on. *Never* get comfortable and think you are at *your* best, and that there shouldn't be any *changes* done to you because you feel as if who you are is *enough*! We're all a work in *progress*! Every day we should *better* ourselves and become better than who we were yesterday.

Your environment *cannot* change until you start making changes within yourself. Your *attitude* changes your point of view of your environment. Stop waiting on a *feeling*! Stop living out of your *flesh* and *emotions* and start living with *determination* and *faith*!

When you settle for *less*, you're actually putting a *discount* on yourself for that other person. Now they won't see the *real* value of you because of that. Why be with someone who has *less* or *no* value compared to you? If you have *high* standards, they should too. Don't *downgrade* for someone just to be fair and accepting. You *deserve* one of God's *best* candidates! Be with someone who reflects you and has the same morals and standards!

Sugarcoating things and beating around the bush *won't* help people. Letting them continue to live in denial about things *won't* free them from their strongholds. Not saying anything *at all* to encourage and uplift them, you're allowing them to have a slow mental death. If you have the *gift* to lift someone's *spirit* up, *use* it! Everyone doesn't have *real*, *true*, and *honest* people to *reveal* to them what *needs* to be *corrected* in their lives.

I don't want to be on this earth and *not* allow God to lead and guide me. I *don't* want to do my *own* thing. Whatever I may have to *face* now and in the future, I want to be *prepared* and *ready* for it. Whatever it is, I don't want it to be a *surprise* to me. I want to *know* how to handle the situation, how *God* would handle it. Let God continue to mold you from the inside out so you can become the person God *always* meant for you to become.

Uncomfortable means to take chances and get out of your comfort zone if you want to be successful. If you're *not* taking risks, you're *not* stepping out in *faith* in trying new things!

Don't trust no one!

Listen folks, God told us in His Word to *never* put our trust in man. But at the same time, people don't really understand how God operates. He wants us to depend on Him during our tough times. But God knows how to use other people to help you get to where you need to be. People out here are becoming antisocial because of maybe family members, friends, or coworkers that have let them down and disappointed them. That doesn't mean everyone else is going to do the same thing. We are *only* humans. We are *not* perfect. We *will* make mistakes and fall short. We cannot satisfy *everyone* and *everything*. Get that through *your* head! Your *attitude* controls your thoughts, and if you don't have those *two* things together, you're *not* going to see things correctly or have the *proper* understanding.

When you're *chasing* the wrong things, you're actually running from the *right* things that are meant for you to have. Your mind is so *distracted* on other things that you cannot even *see* what God is trying to *show* you. Let alone if God is trying to *tell* you something, you have *too much* noise from world in your ears that you *can't* even *hear* Him. But then you want to turn around and say that God is *not* talking to you and that you can't hear Him. Guess what? You *need* to spend quiet, quality time with Him in *your* Word. Drop *your* own agenda and tend to God's agenda for *your* life! If those things that you were *chasing* were for you, why are you *chasing* them then? Shouldn't it just happen for you because that's what was supposed to happen? Wouldn't it be already preplanned for you to have? Think about that!

Ladies, it's better to let the guy pursue you. You don't have to tell the guy that you're interested, *but* there is a way to show it in *not* such a thirsty way. But true to this fellas, I agree with you guys when you say "How are you supposed to know if that woman is interested in you if they don't tell you?" You're *right* about that! Guys are *not* mind readers! I'm just saying, ladies, whether you're interested in him or *not*, it'll only be *real* if he approaches you. You can be interested in someone *all day* and *all night*, but that doesn't mean that they're interested in you.

Whatever you're trying to do, repeat it over *again* and *again* and *again* until you make it *happen*! What do you do during *hard times*? You must have *faith*. Romans 4:17 says "Call forth those things that be not as though they were." Judge not according to appearances. Don't judge your circumstances and the possibilities for your future based upon what you have now and because of what's going on now. That's *not* the real reality there! If you're going through some hard times now, it has *not* come to stay. It has come to *pass*! You must have *patience* and engage in consistent *action*! Everything we want to happen will *not* always happen when we want it to happen. It won't happen quickly.

No matter how bad it is or how bad it gets, *I'm going to make it*!

If you've been *hurt* in the past or currently hurting right now in this moment, God loves you! He doesn't want to see you *cry*. He doesn't want to see you *hurting*. He doesn't want to see you holding on to *pain*! Release it *now*! Give your anxieties and problems over to Him. He can take care of them! You can't deal with them alone. You need Him! Let God love you. Let God *heal* and *mend* your *broken* heart! God's love is unconditional and everlasting. His love *never* fails. It *never* runs out and *never* runs dry!

Love others *even* when they *do* you wrong! You can still *love* others without being their friend. Show *love* to everyone as God did. There is *no* need to be like the *average* person and act *nasty* or become *bitter*!

Love one another! Anyone that does *not* love does not *know* God because God is *love*!

Your life is so *secure* when it's in God's hands! Do you understand what that means? That means whatever plans God has for you, whatever blessings He has for you, the enemy *cannot* destroy nor take them away! These plans were preplanned before *your* birth. God has *literally* made all things *final*! Get *rid* of that mindset, thinking people can ruin things for you. If you're doing the right things and living *your* life right, God's plan for you *will* prosper and succeed! The *only* person that can get in the way of anything happening is *you*!

Whatever it is that you have *your* mind-set on to accomplish, *stick to it*! Don't worry about *how* you're going to do it, *how* long it is going to take. What if something goes *wrong*? Is everything gonna *work* out? I don't have *this*. I don't have *that*. I need *this*. I need *that*! (Pause) God *will* help you. God is a *way maker*! There's *nothing* our God cannot do! Even when the excitement is *gone*, even when things start to get complicated, if God is still behind the scenes working things out for you, you *keep* on praying and pressing *on*!

Being impatient *can* ruin *opportunities*! Never *rush* what needs to be *developed* first!

The things that you are doing that is against the Bible—is it *worth* it? All I am saying is a sin is a *sin*! No *sin* is greater than the other. Is that temptation *worth* it? Is that addiction *worth* it? Don't get me wrong, people make mistakes and slip up. It says it here in Romans 3:23: "For all have sinned and fall short of the glory of God."

It says in Hebrews 26:18: "Dear friends, if we deliberately continue sinning after we have received knowledge of the truth, there is no longer any sacrifice that will cover these sins."

But the Bible also tells us how whether we are a Christian or *not*, if you know the Word of God or if you just basically know right from wrong and still do wrong, you *will* be punished. In James 4:17 says: "So whoever knows the right thing to do and fails to do it, for him it is sin." It also says it here in Leviticus 26:18: "If after all this you will not listen to me, I will punish you for your sins seven times over."

Everyone knows that sin leads to death. It says it in Romans 6:23: "For the wages of sin is death, but the free gift of God is eternal life in Christ Jesus our Lord."

People, you can resist *sin*! James 4:7 says, "Submit yourselves therefore to God. Resist the devil, and he will flee from you."

Ask God for forgiveness and turn away from *sin* completely! Choose to *not* repeat *sin*! Don't just ask for forgiveness and continue to *sin*! God *will* help you get *through* it! It says in 1 Corinthians 10:13: "No temptation has overtaken you that is not common to man. God is faithful, and he will not let you be tempted beyond your ability, but with the temptation he will also provide the way of escape, that you may be able to endure it."

1 John 1:9 says, "If we confess our sins, he is faithful and just to forgive us our sins and to cleanse us from all unrighteousness."

There is a *reward* for living according to the Word!

Deuteronomy 30:15–16 says, "See, I have set before you today life and good, death and evil. If you obey the commandments of the Lord your God that I command you today, by loving the Lord your God, by walking in his ways, and by keeping his commandments and his statutes and his rules, then you shall live and multiply, and the Lord your God will bless you in the land that you are entering to take possession of it." So the question—is it *worth* it?

God said in His Word to *not* gain approval or acceptance from man. Whatever God says about *you* and *your* situation, that is the *truth*. That is *final*! No one else's words can overrule what the Word says.

If God knows what's best for you, wouldn't it be better to let Him run things? Stop trying to be *your* own God. God knew your ending before *your* beginning. Let Him do His job!

This is for *anyone* who is a *home-wrecker*! Listen, no matter how bad you want that girl or that guy, if God put them with that other person, there is *nothing* you can do to separate them. If you wanna be *nasty*, yes, it's possible to make things *rocky* for them. But just know this, you will *never* end up with that person that you're trying to *steal*. You *cannot* mess up *destiny*! You can continue being a *fool* all you want. You'll just end up single and alone until you die. What goes around comes around. You *will* reap what you sow! I'll end it with that!

I just want to encourage you to *not* give up on what God has placed in *your* heart. Because things haven't happened yet doesn't mean it's *not* going to happen. The enemy *will* try to send all *types* of distractions to run you *off* your course. He knows the *plans* God has for you. That's why he's giving you *such* a hard time. This is the *worst* time to throw in the towel. I believe the *worst* it gets, the *closer* your breakthrough is. It's *not* easy at all. Every day, God is giving us the sufficient grace to get us through our storms. He's leading us through it, holding our hand. We're *not* alone. We're *never* alone. He said He would *never* leave us nor forsake us. He is *always* with us.

Ladies, you are a *jewel*. Don't *ever* allow a man to make you feel otherwise. You are *special*! You are *beautiful*. God has someone special for *you*! Don't look for love in the *wrong* way or with the *wrong* people. Wait on God's *best*! Wait for someone who is going to treat you like the *queen* that you are. You've gone through *too much* pain to keep experiencing the same pain *over* and *over* again. *You deserve better!*

You can't *fully* be yourself with some people. You gotta be one-way with them and one-way *only*! As in you can still be cordial saying "Hello, how are you?" Keep it moving. People still got their own issues to deal with. But that's *not* my problem. I just keep them in prayer and enjoy the rest of my day.

There is *no* human being that is *perfect*! There is *no* relationship that will be *perfect*! Prepare yourself for *any* and *everything* when it comes to a relationship. Being in a relationship calls for, of course, having God first in your life *and* communication, strength, commitment, understanding, patience, and perseverance. Ladies, don't become an easy catch! You say you want somebody *real*. Well, take your sweet time and get to know these men that do confront you. It's *your* heart that's on the line. Stay patient! There's *no* rush! With time, all questions *will* be answered!

You say you deserve *better*, but your actions are saying something else. You're going around hunting for the *right* one when you need to be content being single first so you can choose better mates. Being desperate and thirsty, you're going to overlook the *right* one and fall for the *wrong* one. While you're single, build a relationship with God so He can prompt you when the *right* one has arrived. God communicates in different ways, but you have to give Him 100 percent of your attention so He can give you direction like when to move forward and when to *not* make a move with that person.

Trust me, God knows the *desires* of *your* heart. He wants to bless you with those things. But He wants you to *want* him more than those things. Let Him know that He's *first* in *your* life. He doesn't want you to *always* be thinking about everything else except Him. When you get *your* priorities right, He'll do His end of the bargain.

Spending time with God is a great way to clear out the clutter that's trashing up *your* life. Clutter as in *distractions*, people that don't *belong* in your life, *negative* thoughts, etc., you name it! Get rid of it! Clutter are *hindrances*! You say you can't hear from God, but He *communicates* through His Word. You have to be in the Word! You need to do a summer clean up and *get rid* of things or maybe *people* that are blocking *your* blessings from coming through. How can you hear from God if your mind is *always* on everything else? Will you listen to the *noise* of the world, or will you listen to God's *soft* voice so He can lead and guide you? You have to make changes to get results. Time waits for no man. It's time to reap *your* blessings. So start cleaning up!

Wake up expecting God to bless you! No matter how He does it, just have an attitude of *faith*!

Every day when you wake up, *always* remind yourself where you're heading. Despite of how you may wake up and feel, *you* need to make sure that whatever you do *today* is going to benefit you *tomorrow*. Whatever you do *every day* needs to be things that will help you have a *better* future. Stick to your current plan! Laziness will *hinder* your progress!

Develop Self-Control!

You are *RESPONSIBLE* for your own actions. Whatever you decide to do, it will have a *reaction*. Good or bad, you will *reap* what you *sow*! Be careful in what you *do* to other people. Be careful *who* you hang around with. Be careful what you get yourself *into*. Either way, your *actions* will affect your life in many ways. Make wise decisions!

Those things that you want so *bad*, are you willing to work as *hard* as you need to, to have those things? Don't say you want it but don't have the *motivaton* nor the *determination* to get it. Life doesn't come to you on a silver platter. You *work* for what *you* want. There's no such thing as "microwave" success!

If you can't learn how to be happy *alone*, what makes you think when you get a girlfriend or boyfriend that they're going to bring you happiness? The couples you see walking around smiling, acting lovey-dovey, holding hands, hugging and kissing don't mean *squat*! You don't know what's going on behind *closed* doors away from the public eye. Learn how to love *yourself* first.

Take each day a step at a time. Keep a steady pace. Don't speed up or slow down. Stay focused on what you can do in the now, and God will make a way for everything else. Cast all of your cares on Him. It's *only* so much that we can do, so why *not* let God take care of what we have no power to change? We serve a *big* God!

When others see you as a *nobody*, God sees you as a *somebody*. You were made in His image. So when it's time to be promoted and elevated, it'll happen for you and *not* for them. Watch your attitude toward other people because you just might ruin your own blessings.

A lot of people don't know who they are because they're *too* busy trying to be somebody that they're *not*! Ask God to reveal to you *who* you really are, and from then on, *be yourself!*

Your time is coming! God is still preparing *everything* for you. But you do need to prepare and position yourself for your *blessings*!

God knows the plans that He has for us. We don't know what the future holds. So by having *closed* doors, that's how He can get us to move *forward* and in the right direction. Don't think closed doors lead to a *dead end* and think that's it. A blessing is *always* around the corner!

Men of God, keep your *focus* on God so He can reveal to you the *right* woman. He wants to know if you'll keep Him first in your life! It's all a *test*!

If God blessed you with someone that you could be in a relationship with, that person should *only* bring you into an even more deeper relationship with God. If that relationship is making you distant from God, get your priorities together. God should *always* be number one.

That *right* person will see you as *all* that they've *ever* wanted. Regardless of your flaws! Just being with *you* would mean the *world* to them.

No matter *what* has gotten in the way of your dreams. Keep that dream *alive*! No matter what you have to do to *make* it happen, *make it happen*!

Keep the *faith*! Don't *give up*! *Expect your miracle*!

The minute you give up, you're blessing could be right around the corner. Just hold on. Change is coming! Don't worry about anything!

Quitting shows *weakness*! Pressing forward despite of the obstacles shows true *strength*! Remind yourself why you even started the journey then *stick with it*!

Forget what happened yesterday. God provided you strength for today. Don't worry about tomorrow. God will give you all that you need to make it through your day no matter what your plans are. Whether it's school, work, or just plain errands, you're *covered*! Sleep in peace tonight. You deserve some rest. Don't forget the hard work you've done today. Give yourself some credit!

It's normal to feel uncertain in times of hardship. But knowing that you serve a God that knows your beginning and your ending, gives you peace of mind. He knows exactly where you're at in your life right now, and He has a solution *just for you*!

People will judge you *regardless*! It comes to show their maturity if they can't just first get to know you without making conclusions right off the back about you. Make sure you stay *real* with yourself. Trust me, a lot of people don't even deserve the opportunity to get to know you if they "supposedly" have a negative vibe toward you already. *You are destined for greatness! You are who God created you to be.* The opinions of man are irrelevant when God says *you're everything* to Him.

Letting go of the stresses of life, giving them to God, gives room to have hope, to smile, and to relax. Though this world is full of ups and downs, it's always best to smile from the inside out. Smile for a better future! Things won't always be the same. Seasons are always changing. Things will get better! Do you believe that?

There's only one *you*. Why change and become someone else if God created you to be different and to *stand out*?

In order to get your rainbow, you gotta go through the rain.

Be *yourself*! Everybody can't hang with you. Only those that are meant to be in your life will stay. People come and go. *That's life*! Keep it moving!

What if we came together to build each other up instead of tearing each other down? Where would we be then?

Best thing to do is to sit back, relax, and let God take over your current situations.

I dare you today, go somewhere quiet and be totally and completely alone. Spend some time with God, no time limit and literally pour out your concerns to Him. I mean, just open yourself up completely, no holding back. (Even if that means you start to cry.) It's just you and God. Talk to Him as if He's your homeboy or homegirl. Just simple talking, nothing fancy. Just be yourself. He doesn't judge. His Word says in James 4:8: "Draw close to God, and God will draw close to you." Psalm 142:2–3 says, "I pour out my complaints before God and tell him all my troubles. For I am overwhelmed." Just by you even talking to Him is putting a smile on His face. Just vent out all that is bothering you and that is weighing you down. After you're done, *let it go*!

Before you go to bed tonight, don't end your night mad or stressed out. Whatever it is, *let it go*! Go to bed with nothing but peace. It's a brand-new day tomorrow. Wake up refreshed!

Look forward to becoming a *better* person. Don't go back to the person you used to be. Change your life for the better. No matter what others say, be who God created you to be. No one is perfect. We've all sinned and made mistakes. Who cares! Don't allow people to bring up your past just to tear you down from becoming a better *you*. Your past does not *define* who *you* are! The choices *you* make now is what will *define* you. Make good choices starting *today*!

When dating, show a person how serious you are about your celibate walk, and they will show you how serious they are about you.

We don't deserve *anything*, yet God gives us *everything*!

Everybody can't go where you're going so just *walk alone*. Only you can walk down your own road. There will be people that you meet along the way to boost you forward, but at the end of day, it's just you and God.

Worrying and having anxiety are both attacks on the mind. Worrying is useless. It does not accomplish any good thing. In Philippians 4:6, God says, "Cast all of your cares and anxieties upon him." In that case, why worry and why be so anxious?

If you're always looking for advice, motivation, or encouragement from someone, guess what? You're not going to *always* get it. You need to *motivate* and *encourage* yourself. Don't wait for other people. You got goals to accomplish. This is *your* year!

Listen, *don't ever* walk around and say you got everything on your own with no help. Whatever you do have is only because God allowed you to have those things. Don't ever give yourself all the credit. A matter of fact, you get *no credit at all*! I don't care if you got a car, job, or your own place. God gave you connections to be able to even have those things. You don't have to be a Christian or "saved" for God to want to bless you. He just wants a relationship with you in return. Is that too much to ask for, after all He has done for you? Priceless isn't it? Yeah. So if you wanna be *big-headed* and claim all of your hard work on yourself, God doesn't mind taking back all that He has blessed you with. He wants all the credit, brownie points, and kudos. He's the One that should get all of the appreciation. We as people just need to be *grateful*! So no matter how much money you got, clothes you wear, and all that materialistic stuff you are flashing around in people's faces and on social media websites, *all of that* can be *gone* sooner than you think. *Get your priorities right*!

Your past does not determine who you are. Your past prepares you for who you are to become. God has given you a new beginning—a fresh start.

Stay focused on the road ahead of you. Stop looking in the rearview mirror!

People will talk about you whether you're doing good or bad! Keep walking.

You have not reached your limits. This is not as good as it gets. Your greatest victories are still out in front of you!

Someone's opinion of you doesn't have to become your reality!

For anything that made you cry today can make you smile tomorrow! God has more for you!

Don't let anyone's "no" stop what God has said "yes" to you about!

People will always feel the need to give their opinion or criticize you when you're trying to do something positive for yourself or in your life. It's only because they don't know the plans that God has for you. But it's not for them to know. It's for you to make sure those plans come to pass. Ignore the noise and listen for God's voice!

Faith is not just a feeling or a thought. It is a lifestyle!

Never give up on yourself. You are far more important than you have ever imagined!

Often "old friends" don't understand the "new change" in you. You are being used for a purpose!

You don't need to have a man or woman to show or give you love. God can give you all the love you could ever need. His love is like no other because *He is love*!

When people are finished with you, God is just getting started!

God calls ordinary people to do extraordinary things. It is God that decides, not man!

Some people will never be happy with your decisions. You must ask yourself if you are trying to please man or trying to please God!

Don't try to force open what God has determined that needs to be closed off!

Speak blessings out of your mouth, not curses. Speak joy, peace, love, healing, and a financial breakthrough over your life. Think on things that are pure, holy, lovely, honest, just, and of good report, not on things that are negative, evil, discouraging, sin, impurity, and that is not of God. Whatever God hates, so should you. Whatever God loves, so should you. Be more like Jesus Christ!

Don't just stay stuck talking about "God will make a way." He'll make a way when you walk. It's called the faith walk, not the faith couch potato!

Tough times don't last—tough people do! Remember God is on your side!

Sometimes, pleasing God means disappointing people! In the end, there is a great reward for a life of obedience!

Everybody goes through something that changes them in a way that they can never go back to the person they once were! Allow the lessons of life to make you better, not bitter!

We all have our temporary weak moments. *But* don't let those weak moments turn *permanent*! At the end of the day, *yes*, we are humans, and we do have emotions. But what's *dangerous* is that our thoughts and emotions can affect our performance and how we react to certain situations. Don't *lose* hope! Keep the *faith*! Don't *give up*!

Don't waste your time explaining who you are to people who are committed to misunderstanding you.

You must find the courage to show up for the fight. Remember, God is with you!

Surround yourself with people who will help build your destiny! A true friend sees your potential!

Stop wasting your time defending yourself. Those that do not understand where you are coming from probably won't understand where you are trying go!

Never let *anyone* use where you've been to discredit where you are! People will always try to use your past against you when you begin to do better. Let them know you've done your time and been *paroled* from your past.

Don't allow yourself to believe that *change* is an overnight process! Before change begins, you have to be *tired*! You have to turn around and face Satan and say, "I'm tired of getting high, tired of getting locked up, tired of being in this situation or relationship, tired of this lifestyle, tired of not knowing my purpose or progress." Then turn to the *Lord* and say, "I'm ready for change!" The final step is to be patient. Keep seeking self-betterment and watch *him* work.

Remember, you are filled with endless potential and possibilities!

Have you ever noticed that *every time* you accomplish something, people speak negative about you or you lose friends? Don't be mad or frustrated, just learn that everyone hasn't been authorized to go where *God* is taking you.

To endure means to stand firm under pressure. God will strengthen you in your struggle!

Embrace the beauty of every moment. Live life to the fullest!

Don't settle for less when God has someone who accepts your past, supports your present, loves you, and encourages your future.

In order to get what you want, you must have the courage to get rid of what you don't want! With God, you can let it go!

Don't forget to pray before you lay. Let God know that you're grateful that He has blessed you to see another day! So many of us take life for granted. But so many leave this earth too early. Expect a better day tomorrow and another breath!

Start your day off with positive thoughts. Yesterday is in the past now. Today is a new day! Focus on the present (right now). Don't worry about tomorrow! Be determined to enjoy your today!

God uses people to bless your life, and He will use *your life* to be a blessing as well!

You cannot look ahead and look behind you at the same time! You're either going to look toward your future with faith or stay stuck in your past with doubts. Your choice!

WHO WERE YOU YESTERDAY?

If you really want to do something, you will find a way; if you don't, you will find an excuse!

God will always give you another chance. The choice is yours to take. He loves you very much!

You have not finished the best part of your life. There is more to do!

Today, remember you are who God says you are, and you can do what God says you can do!

Make room for your tomorrow by saying good-bye to your yesterday!

For every problem, God has a solution. You don't conquer a mountain without a climb!

Today is a great day for God to do something *big* in your life! Just *believe*.

You are only limited by what you allow yourself to believe. With God, anything is possible!

Keep your head up today because God is on your side. He has your back!

The love that God has for you is unconditional.

Don't let the enemy rob you of good moments in the present because of bad moments in the past. Your past does *not* determine who you are or where you are going!

People can sense when you are going somewhere and not everyone wants you to get there. But you have God!

You cannot control the circumstances around you, but you can control how you respond or react.

Don't worry about the trouble today. You have God on your side. You will smile tomorrow!

Face the day with the trust that God is on your side!

Don't compare yourself to everyone around you. You're a Designer's original!

No matter what storms you've been going through, I'm here to let you know that soon it'll get much better and easier. Do you believe that? Because I do.

Stop living by what you feel and live by what God says! You are who God says you are!

The only job you have is to believe God can do His job!

You can't just have faith. You must *operate in faith*!

You can't just like God or want God. You must *need* God!

Never waste time on getting *revenge*. Those people who hurt you will eventually face their own karma!

God will always give you another chance: the choice is yours to take it.

When people want to control you, they will try to reduce you in order to raise themselves up. *But God is on your side!*

Sometimes you just need to go somewhere new and start over fresh. Maybe if things aren't really working out, God is directing you to another place where your blessing is. To be honest, I think that's what He wants me to do. I might just do that. More opportunities in other areas. If this status pertains to you, pray about it. It won't hurt to try something new, especially if it's something God wants you to do.

Take the time to talk to God, not just pray but speak to Him. Let Him know how you are feeling!

Tough times do not last—tough people do! Stand firm in the Lord!

Faith is not always expecting the best to happen but accepting that whatever happens is always for the best!

Make a decision to think on the things of God today and see how situations turn around!

Today, know that God will provide the strength to get through.

Whatever your fear is, you can overcome it—be facing it head-on with the power of Christ!

Faith is not just a feeling or a thought. It is a lifestyle! Start living by it today!

God did not create us to feel bad or barely make it. He created us to walk in joy and live a Spirit-filled life.

You are not who people say you are. You are who God says you are! He says you can succeed! He says you can have a future that is blessed!

God's favor will open doors and create opportunity. Undeserved access!

You have been chosen by God. Don't try to rush His plan for your life. Trust in His timing!

Write down your goals, not only to remind yourself but to declare *boldly* to the enemy that you are serious about achieving it!

Don't worry if someone won't let you "play in their sandbox." God will build you a whole playground!

Whatever God has promised, He is faithful to fulfill it!

Try to take something in today. Refresh yourself physically and spiritually. You can't always just give out. You have to replenish.

Stand firm on God's Word. Even in the darkest days, God has you. He will vindicate you. He will fight for you!

You can't praise God and be frustrated at the same time. Devote yourself to praising Him and give your cares over!

Through your faith and courage, God will make the impossible possible!

Do not allow worries for your future to prevent you from trusting God. Trust in His timing!

If God has shown you a vision to achieve, rest assured, He will bless you with all the resources you need to make it come to pass!

The enemy ultimately wants you to lose your position by intimidation, insecurity, and jealousy. Remember, you have God on your side!

Even before anybody else accepted you, God accepted you! Before anybody else loved you, God loved you!

Don't get upset if somebody gives you a hard time today. Don't get upset if you don't get your way or if somebody says or does something you don't like. If you are set up for an upset, stay stable. It is only a test.

Your failure is never final with God! Get up and go forward knowing that He uses the "pits" in your life to promote you to the "palace"

Fight the enemy by declaring the Word! Speak God's Word and watch the enemy run!

Don't let anyone rain on your parade! Keep dreaming. Keep believing, and keep celebrating each step of victory! God is faithful!

No matter what you may be going through, God would not put more on you than you can handle. If God brought you to it, then He will bring you through it. Jesus says to cast your cares upon him. Lay aside every weight that is in your life. There are other ways to enjoy life. We don't have to struggle.

Give your cares over to God. He will fight for you. He is your strength! You don't have to feel you are in the battle alone.

Don't make someone a first choice who makes you a last one!

When you live from vision, you let your future control your decisions and not your past!

It is *never* too late to pursue God's purpose for your life, no matter what your current situation is!

Refuse to be agitated, disturbed, and upset today. Instead, be of good cheer: take courage; be confident, certain, and undaunted. The enemy wants your day to go downhill. Don't let him take control of your day. Show him who's your boss—Jesus Christ!

You were designed by God "perfect," according to His purpose! Not to "man's standard," but God's standard! Lift your head up and keep moving!

Recognize that no other human being can ever complete you! *Only God* can do that!

I can't *complain*! God has been good *all around*!

I know that I make it through anything because I am determined to *overcome* all that may come my way. With God, I am *victorious*!

Prayer and having faith changes things.

If you're ever unsure about something, *just ask*! There is *no* reason to have to wonder, to be curious or confused about anything. Save the *frustration* and locate the Source to provide the correct answers.

Lord, I give you all of my worship and praise! I give you *everything*! Nothing can separate me from your love!

I am *excited* because I know that things are getting *better*! Your attitude is *everything*!

Stay humble. Be content, thankful, and grateful for what you have. Then God will *elevate* you, *increase* everything that you have, and *bless* you with more!

There isn't a dream that you can't make to come true. The magic is your *determination*!

I'm doing all that I can to live a *better* life. I am expecting *every* area of my life to get better. I am *not* quitting until God blesses me! And once He does, I'm still going to keep pressing so He can keep blessing!

That door you just closed allowed another door to open with *better* opportunities! Be confident and walk through it. It's *for you*!

There's *no* room for procrastination and laziness when it comes to being successful. You better have some dirty hands when you make it to the *top*!

I just want to encourage someone who may be dealing with some type of health issue or know of someone that is currently facing health issues, big or small. Back in biblical times, if God performed miracles such as making the blind to see, the deaf to hear, the lame to walk, the lepers to be cured, and the dead to be brought back to life (Matthew 11:4–6), there is *no* health situation too hard for God. Always remember, there is somebody dealing with a worse health issue(s) than you. Also, there are people who have had a worse health issue than you and were *healed*! Believe that God doesn't want to see you suffering in any kind of way. He allows things to happen for a reason. There is a lesson in everything that we face. You have to discover what that is and apply it to your life. But trust and have faith that He *will* finish what these doctors and surgeons *couldn't*!

Never have yourself revolving around other people. Like for example, "Whatever they do determines what you do" kind of thing. *Focus* on keeping yourself *first*, not in a selfish way but just making sure you do what makes you *happy*! People can't always *satisfy* us, so let's satisfy *ourselves*! We *know* what we *want*, and we can *provide* it on our own.

Trust God with your situation, no matter how big or small it is, and watch Him turn things around for your good!

People that *never* give up are the ones that get what they worked *hard* for!

I believe if we *all* supported each other without making *everything* a jealousy thing or a competition, that we *all* would make it to the top *together*!

There is *nothing* that you can't do unless you tell yourself that you can't do it!

There's *nothing* wrong with sharing your accomplishments to family, friends, coworkers, or strangers, but just know that everybody *won't* be happy for you. So you really don't have to say anything at all. Your accomplishments will speak for themselves. Your life will showcase your results!

Don't spend another day trying to convince someone of your worth! If they can't discern it, they don't deserve it!

Stop looking for something on the outside to *fix* what's on the inside! Allow God's love to pierce through the pain and heal any hurt!

Hate is very educational. When you discover what others hate and reject in you, you discover what makes you so valuable.

God is your Source, the source of your strength, your peace, your joy! Speak to Him. Pray to Him. Cry out to Him!

Don't give your time, energy, and attention to something that is not going to matter in a few years! Focus on what is important to your destiny.

God can take any situation, repair it, and restore it when He is invited to do so!

God is *for you*! He has a good plan for your life and *that plan will prevail!*

Cut off everything that is cutting off life in you!

Don't count other people's blessing! God has a tailor-made blessing with *your* name on it!

Everybody likes a shortcut, but faster results aren't always better! Trust in God. Rest in Him!

God is preparing you for what He has already prepared for you! *Get ready!*

Remember, God has a purpose and a plan. His perfect plan is always at work, and *you* are part of that plan.

Trust in God's timing. We become impatient and in panic, but God is *never* late! He is always right on time!

Surrendering to change means letting go of control! Trust that God has a better tomorrow for you, with good plans to give you an expected end!

Remember God has a purpose and a plan. His perfect plan is always at work, and *you* are part of that plan!

Trust in God's timing. We become impatient and in panic, but God is *never* late! He is always right on time!

Close your eyes, take a deep breath, and remind yourself that you're not alone. God is right there with you.

Nobody is perfect. But at the end of the day, we are all adults, and we know right from wrong. Make better decisions is what I'm saying.

Don't wait until things get bad for that to be a "news flash" for you to get your life together to make better choices! Do it now!

When you belong to Christ, things that appear to be a "setback" become a "setup" for something far greater than you expected.

Never give up on something you can't go a day without thinking about. *God is able!*

Even when you don't feel like it, trust God enough and believe in your dream enough to keep moving toward it!

Don't try to predict your end from your beginning! You can't look forward and backward at the same time! Stay on course!

You gotta stay productive every day. That's the only way to make progress to reach your goals. Long as you procrastinate, you will become lazy, and you won't get anywhere!

Nothing is impossible. Anything can happen. Although you can't see the big picture, it doesn't mean it's not there. Things will eventually reveal itself in due time.

Don't be passive about what you truly want. Go after it and claim what's yours!

Decide to be part of the solution, not part of the problem!

You can't move into the future God has for you with things that are weighing you down from your past! Let it go, forgive, and move forward!

You don't know when someone can come into your life and change it forever! God has divine setups for you!

The only mistakes you can learn from are the ones you survive. Falling down is not failing, staying down is! Get back up by the grace of God!

Don't hold on to anything that will hinder or hold back your blessing! Trust that God has more ahead of you than anything behind you!

Real relationships and true friends accept your past, support your present, love you, and encourage your future. Find those that fit!

Do you know how many people don't get a chance to see a beautiful new day as this? We're blessed to be alive right now. Be grateful!

Stop worrying. Nothing in your life can catch God off guard. He has already made a plan for every obstacle in your life, and He'll take care of you.

No matter who rejects you, God accepts you.

Set your mind on things that are above, and let go of worry, fear, doubt, and unbelief.

I want you to know that God loves you, and He'll never leave you! No matter what you've done in the past or what you're doing now, He accepts you for who you are. Let Him love you today!

I am a woman of worth, and I deserve the best.

Embrace who you are. You have been given every tool, every talent, every trait you need to realize your destiny. You can't be everything to everyone. All you can be is *you*. And that is enough. Take criticism from the crowd as a compliment.

You can't lose unless you forfeit or give up! So keep fighting for what you believe in and make it happen!

You cannot revive something that God says is not going to work! Don't be afraid to let go. There is something better ahead of you!

Have *big* dreams because you have a *big* God!

Fight for your righteousness *every day*!

Don't ever change who you are for anyone or anything. Change only certain things about you that could be negative to become an even better, more positive person. Make the change for yourself!

When you have peace on the inside, you have peace on outside! Don't let anyone or anything steal your peace. You need it!

Take a deep breath, relax, and enjoy your day! Today will be a great day for you.

Treat today as if it was your last. Don't let little things ruin your day so easily!

When you have patience, you will get what you deserve at the right time in the right way. When you don't have patience, you will get what you weren't supposed to get at a bad time in a bad way! Just pray and ask God for a full load of patience. It will help you in the long run in life!

Whatever you want in life, *go* and *get it*! Don't expect for it to be given to you and you didn't work for it! Don't rely on anyone or anything to help you out either because people nowadays are only looking out for themselves. So at the end of the day, make sure you are looking out for you and become *independent*!

Just because you have brains and connections doesn't make you successful. God gave you that brain and those connections. Who's getting all the credit?

Need a blessing? Ask God.

Step out in faith today. Take the first step. God will meet you!

Ask God for the strength and courage to face and overcome your pain by forgiving those that have harmed you. You don't have to live a second longer with that burden!

My praises go up, blessings come down!

Trust in God! Nothing is impossible with Him!

If you are not happy on the inside, there is *nothing* on the outside that will make you happy!

Never regret your choices in life because even the bad ones lead to good lessons.

God has *empowered* you! You have been *empowered* to succeed and prosper!

Right now, take your worry and transform it into prayer. Go!

They said you "could not," but they left out the *God factor*! *You can do all things* through Christ Jesus!

The details and decisions of your life will fall into place if your heart is in the right place, and that's what "God's will" is all about.

No matter how much hatred us humans have toward each other, at the end of the day, we were put on this earth to love one another and to support each other!

Looks and sizes don't matter! *You are beautiful, embrace your beauty!*

Life will get hard, but let the pain inspire you to run *to* God and *not from* God!

Always put your trust in God!

You were created completely unique. God designed you to be *you*. And He has a specific purpose for you!

Falling down is *not* failure, staying down is! Start celebrating your failures as getting one step closer to your victory!

Within a negative world, be that positive light, and let it rub off on others!

Never invest your time into ignorant people; invest in positive, successful people! You'll get better results!

Less time to be stressed; more time to be blessed!

The love of God has no limits.

If we change our thoughts, we can change our outcomes.

Don't fall asleep with problems on your mind. Pray before you lay!

When you're confused about something, seek God. He will surely let you know what's up.

The devil may try to mess up your morning, but speak life, and let him know he won't take your joy away today!

Love yourself because you're beautiful, loved, and important to God. Don't you ever forget that.

All of us fail. But we don't have to live in failure. Get up.

Forgiveness equals freedom! Forgive others, but don't forget to forgive yourself as well. You are not burdened by your past!

If someone randomly walks into your life, find out their intentions because you won't know what their plans are for you! Don't just trust anybody. Nowadays, you can't trust nobody but God!

Block out all negativity today. That's the only way to have a good, positive day.

God is saying "Let's start by getting order in your life. Let's prioritize."

Whatever the curse is, whatever the dysfunction, whatever has plagued you, with God, it can be broken!

There is no dream too big for those that truly believe in the power of God!

The favor of God will take you where you cannot take yourself!

Trust God. He will never fail you, forsake you, or leave you!

Don't try to get from a person what only God can give you!

I pray that blessings, goodness, favor, and prosperity overtake you in Jesus' name! You will recover all the enemy has stolen!

Forgive those who hurt you. Forget what went wrong but remember what God wanted you to learn and what it taught you!

You are not a product of your past. You are a product of God! Your mistakes are meant to guide you, not define you!

Be grateful of the things God has blessed you with. Thank God tonight before you go to bed for His many blessings that He has bestowed upon your life.

Just know that your struggles are over. God is going to take that pressure off of you. He is going to give you deliverance. Be strong!

Everything will change. Nothing will stay the same! God can turn your life around sooner than you think. Just say the word and believe in His Word!

Don't lose hope. When you are down to nothing, God is up to something.

When you want to see the mountain in your life removed—pray!

God had the solution before you ever faced the problem!

If you are governed by the Holy Spirit, letting someone "have it" shouldn't make you feel better (even when they deserve it).

The more you look up to God, the less you will look down on people.

Don't worry about what's going on around you. Focus on you and only you! Let everyone else go on their own path. Everyone is going their separate ways anyway. You can't follow down someone else's path. Each path is specifically for one person. We all get to where we're going differently. So stay in your lane! Things will work out!

Stop allowing your past to interfere with your future.

In the end, it's not going to matter how many times you fell down but how many times you got back up! God is your strength!

Although there are people out in the world trying to ruin your day or maybe your life, just remember you have control over that! Don't give anyone that kind of power! If anything, they walked in, but you can kick them out! Your life, your happiness! Make it happen! Have a good day!

When you have God in your heart, it truly shows! Others will definitely see it and feel it! So let God use you!

If God brings you to it, He will bring you through it!

Your self-esteem should not be derived from how great you think you are but from how much God loves you.

Feed your faith, starve your fear, and kill your flesh!

God has already gone before you and made a way where there was no way! Don't worry or stress out, *trust Him!*

If you are still alive, God is not done with you yet!

The key to getting along with others is having the mind of Christ.

If people can anger you, they can control you. So don't give anyone that power!

Sometimes it takes the things that don't last forever to teach us the lessons that will.

If we depend on Christ for everything, we can endure anything!

To be found, you must admit you are lost!

When you put your fear behind you, you are capable of succeeding with no distractions.

God, give us the strength to face our problems and not try to flee from them.

Faith connects our weakness to God's strength!

Faith helps us accept what we cannot understand!

You are headed in the right direction when you walk with God.

If you made your mind up that you're going to be a certain way or think a certain way from now on, don't allow anyone to come around and change that decision!

Keep your eyes on the Lord, and you won't lose sight of life's purpose!

Whenever you start to feel like you're weak in any situation, remind yourself that you are strong because God's grace is sufficient!

We are all made in the image of God. We are His work of art. His masterpiece. We are all unique in His creation!

No one can ever amount to God's love. His love is far more superior than any human love!

Regardless of your situation, you can choose to praise the Lord!

The seeds we sow today determine the kind of fruit we'll reap tomorrow.

We worship God for who He is and not because of what we'll get. When we acknowledge what we owe, we'll thank Him that He paid our debt!

The devil is always trying to take away your joy and happiness, but you have to let Him know who's in charge!

When you feel like giving up, think twice cause there's always somebody that needs you, somebody that loves you, and looks up to you. Look at yourself in the mirror and tell yourself, "I can do this. God got me! I won't give up now." Be encouraged.

Being a Christian doesn't mean I'm better than you! It simply means I have a sincere, passionate, honest, burning desire to not sin!

Delay is not denial, so keep praying.

When doors just keep closing, that is just God saying, "Go in another direction. That's not what I want for you."

Love is deaf. You can't just tell someone you love them. You have to show them.

Don't let a great opportunity slip through your fingers. Pursue it and give all the effort you got to make it work!

Your relationship with God is more important than anything because you know for sure that's a relationship that will last forever.

God does not care about your past. Hold His hand and watch the Holy Spirit manufacture and establish your future!

From now on, let Jesus be the center of your focus. Everyday!

Promotion may not come when you want it to, but it will come if you remain faithful.

Ask God to help you look forward toward your future, not backwards where you're past is!

God's miracles never cease to amaze us!

If God answers your prayers, He is increasing your faith. If He doesn't, He is training your patience.

Success will only come if God is your business partner!

God will strengthen you and encourage you when nobody else will!

Life is too short to spend it trying to keep others happy. You cannot please everyone. Keep your focus on pleasing God.

God loves us too much to allow us to stay tied to anyone or anything that does not bring out the best in us.

Let God be the last person on your mind before you go to bed! Lord, watch over us as we sleep. Protect us and give us another day to see. Amen.

Count your blessings daily. You have more than you realize!

It's good to learn of our weakness if it drives us to lean on God's strength.

Life doesn't come with a remote, get up, and change it yourself!

Approach this new week *expecting* nothing but *good* news!

No matter what you're facing, you're going to make it anyhow!

Your determination determines how far you will go. What you put in is what you'll get out! Your results will be from your *actions!*

Trust God with your situation, no matter how *big* or small it is, and watch Him turn things around for your good.

People that *never* give up are the ones that get what they worked *hard* for!

There's *nothing* wrong with sharing your accomplishments to family, friends, coworkers, or strangers, but just know that everybody *won't* be happy for you. So you really don't have to say anything at all. Your accomplishments will speak for themselves. Your life will showcase your results!

Some people just don't want to see you be *great*. You will just have to *disappoint* them!

I believe, if we *all* supported each other without making *everything* a jealousy thing or a competition, that we *all* would make it to the top *together*!

God is preparing you for *greater* endeavors! You will have a *major* impact on others!

There is *nothing* that you can't do unless you tell yourself that you can't do it!

If God is *not* making a big deal about your situation, neither should *you*!

We give up too easily because we're impatient. But we need to have patience in order to see results! Accept the fact that in order to see change, it may take some time.

When God is in it, whatever that you're trying to do, it doesn't matter if people don't understand you or want to support you. God understands and will support you. He will make it happen with or without them!

Pray, believe, wait, receive!

We all have a gift or talent that should be used. It could be part of your purpose in life! Discover it and use it!

Only look back to remember how far you've come but focus on what's ahead because that's where you belong.

I will not be a wasted vessel for God's will for my life!

When you're *ambigious* about a dream or a goal and need people to help, that's when you find out who your *true* supporters are!

Get *excited* and believe that things are getting *better*! Your attitude is *everything*!

As long as you're doing something, you should see *progress*! Forget how long it may take or what *all* you may have to do. Just *do something* toward what's concerning you.

Keep pushing! Those obstacles will eventually move out the way!

Whether you see it or not, have faith!

When you're faced with issues beyond your control, God has already worked it out! He's way ahead of you!

When God blesses you, don't forget about Him. Keep Him first!

Don't allow anyone or anything to block your blessings. It's not worth the loss!

It is an awesome experience to see God's promises being fulfilled in our lives!

Our lives are affected by our attitude, thoughts, actions, and quality of life!

You have to motivate yourself and not wait for feelings to come!

If you stay humble and content, God will continue to bless you!

Less thinking, more doing!

Instead of thinking about your current problems, think about your current blessings!

Make the best out of what you have right now. More is on its way!

If you believe, then you'll achieve!

Faith connects our weakness to God' strength!

Faith helps us accept what we cannot understand!

Less time to be stressed, more time to be blessed!

Never invest your time into ignorant people; invest in positive, successful people! You'll get better results!

Feed your faith, starve your fears, and kill your flesh!

Don't try to get from a person what God can only give you!

God had the solution before you ever faced the problem!

Focus on what really matters to you instead of other people's opinions!

Never let anything or anyone ruin your day. Learn to control your emotions and thoughts. That person or situation is over for a reason. So continue enjoying life! Better things and people are on the way. Patience is the key!

When someone treats you like an option, help them narrow their choices by removing yourself from the equation.

You have to be optimistic about the desires of your heart. Because when what you want or need hasn't happened yet, it doesn't mean you can't be excited while you wait. You know it's going to eventually happen so just be positive and have patience! Everything will work out just fine! Cheer up!

People are always going to be try to tear you down because you're different. Let them know that they can never change you. You are unique in God's eyes.

God will answer your prayers. But you have to believe, have faith and patience. If you don't, you will start doubting His works. Nothing will happen once you start doubting. If you struggle with that, ask God to help you overcome that and to give you complete strength.

Let God's word fill your memory, rule your heart, and guide your life.

I rather be patient and wait on the Lord than try to make things work on my own knowing that everything could fall apart!

Just because you can't see the air doesn't mean you stop breathing. And just because you can't see God doesn't mean you should stop believing!

When the world around you is crumbling, God is the Rock on which you can stand!

You have to take those first steps of *forgiveness* to experience *freedom*! It is time to move on!

God speaks through His Word, take time to listen.

We all have our struggles, don't give up! Stay prayed up and think positive! No matter what you're going through! You can make it, you can do it!

Listening to Jesus is the first step to following Him.

Where you are is not where you're supposed to stay. God has new levels. Get a bigger vision.

Stop living to please everybody else. Follow your own heart and really do what you believe that God wants you to do.

Be who God created you to be, not who your friends want you to be!

You might not know the exact route to success but it doesn't mean to give up and stop making moves. A door will eventually open for you. Let God handle that. You keep doing your part, and He'll do His!

To develop a personal relationship with God means to learn to love what He loves and hate what He hates.

God gives His hardest battles to His toughest soldiers.

If you live for people's acceptance, you'll die from their rejection.

The devil may come at you while you're weak, but Jesus is the One that you'll seek.

We can't cleanse our own hearts; only God can do that. If we confess our sins to Him, He promises to make us totally clean!

When you know God is about to bless you, you can't help it but *get excited*!

If we use the Word of God to help us make decisions, maybe we wouldn't make so many mistakes in our lives!

Feed your faith, starve your fears, and kill your flesh!

Don't try to get from a person what God only give you!

If you work on something long enough, you will see a difference!

With or without support, follow the passion that burns within!

When you have God, you have everything you need!

Don't wish your life was easier. Just be stronger than your circumstances!

I know what I don't have. But, Lord, I'm thanking you for what I do have!

Don't stress over anyone or anything when you've done all that you could do! As of right now, *faith* is all you have! Use it!

If you knew who were in Christ, you wouldn't try to be someone that you're not. You would be who God created you to be!

You have to keep moving forward or you'll never get to where you want to be. Stopping will only prolong your arrival!

No matter what you are currently facing right now, God is about to place you in a better position in your life!

You have to believe that God has good intentions whenever you are going through tough times. You may not like the process, but the outcome is worth it!

Choose to wait for the right things instead of rushing into the wrong things. Having patience will help you avoid unnecessary stress.

Expect this week to be better than last week! Change your attitude if need be! In order to get better results, you have to switch it up!

Stand out and be different, or you'll never be noticed or discovered!

Become your *biggest* competition! Challenge yourself *daily*! Never *quit*. Never *give up*! Always have *goals* so you can always stay in *motion*!

When you *stop* focusing on other people and start focusing *more* on yourself, that's when you'll start to *mature* and *grow*!

When going through tests and trials, it will *never* be an enjoyable journey. But it does help with mental, emotional, and spiritual development. Good things do come out of bad experiences!

Just know when you pray, you're bound to get a response back in some kind of way whether you like the response or not. After that, it's up to you what you want you do next!

Life gets a little easier to bear when you allow God to help out and *not* take on the stresses of the world all on your own!

Just know God has amazing plans for you! You are *not* on this earth without a purpose!

When you're in a difficult situation, just think of it as another experience you will get through!

No matter what you're facing right now, *never* stop counting your blessings!

You may not like where you are but be determined to get to where you want to be!

Don't worry! God will work everything out just like He always do!

Don't allow your current situation to determine your future! "Right now" is only temporary!

Just because you don't know a way out of your situation doesn't mean that there isn't a way at all! God will provide you a solution! Be patient!

Praying, having faith and patience has a lot to do with you receiving your blessing!

Sometimes when we need to make a move, we don't! That's when opportunities pass us by, and we won't know when we'll get another chance!

Stay positive no matter how your day begins, what happens during your day, or how your day ends!

Keep working toward what you want so that one day you can say you *have it*!

If you know what your purpose is on this earth, you need to be operating in it now! Someone out there is looking for someone with your kind of gifts! Don't let them go to waste, and don't let yourself or others discourage you in using them either!

The more good you *give out*, the more good you'll *receive*!

It may be *difficult*, but it's not *impossible*!

Sometimes we focus on *how long* something will take which can *discourage* us! Focus on reaching that goal no matter what!

People that are *successful* are the ones that never took *no* for an answer and sure didn't quit either!

Learn to *adapt* to any *environment* or *situation* that you may be placed in. That's how you *survive*!

Whatever you can't do on your own, God will help you do it for you! Either way, it's going to happen!

No need to stress when you have someone who can do *all* things!

Even if you get to the point where you've reached all of your goals, *never* stop working toward something! Stay driven to continue making a difference in your life or lives around you!

You can't always rush everything. Some things just need to naturally happen on its own!

We're all going to have problems but don't become the one creating them!

Don't sit back and watch someone *do* what you would like to do. *Get up* and do it too!

Stay focused! This world is full of distractions!

About the Author

BREAUNNA DANIELS WAS BORN and raised in Miami, Florida, but is currently residing in Jacksonville, Florida. She is the youngest of two daughters and is a proud aunt of her first niece. Breaunna started writing at the age of nineteen. Her first novel is entitled *Who Were You Yesterday?*

She is the founder of SoulChic Speaks, which is a motivational fan page that was created in 2012 where she posts inspirational quotes for daily enrichment. You can follow her motivational fan pages at Facebook.com/SoulChicSpeaks, Instagram: @SoulChicSpeaks, and Twitter: @SoulChicSpeaks.

Breaunna is exploring and mainstreaming the importance of self-preservation. She has a background in the health care industry involving health care management and pharmacy technology. She desires to cultivate her dream as a public motivational speaker. Her passion, spirit, and worship for the Lord are actively increasing. Breaunna plans to publish more novels in the future. Ideally, she plans to spread encouragement to others through Christ around the world to all ages and ethnicities.

CPSIA information can be obtained
at www.ICGtesting.com
Printed in the USA
LVHW091337251019
635347LV00001B/6/P